A new book in
THE JOSSEY-BASS SERIES
IN HIGHER EDUCATION

COOPERATIVE EDUCATION IN COMMUNITY COLLEGES

Go to work or go to college? This is no longer an either-or proposition. The driving force separating labor and education is collapsing as programs that emphasize the benefits of both are integrated in college curriculums. Within ten years, one expert predicts, fully 25 per cent of all community college students will enroll in cooperative education programs. This new sourcebook is devoted to the growing cooperative education movement in community colleges and other two-year schools.

Cooperative Education in Community Colleges clearly demonstrates that cooperative education is ideally suited to the broad purpose of community colleges, to breaking down the artificial barrier between college and community, and to diminishing the distinction between education and work. The author outlines procedures for designing and organizing programs and for recruiting employers; defines the roles of instructors, counselors, and administrators;

shows how to promote programs to students and the community; and provides a detailed, "how-to-do-it" model of a comprehensive community college program. Heermann examines the philosophies of vocational and general cooperative education; presents organizational alternatives; and offers administrators developing new cooperative projects a whole series of forms and records useful for such a task. And for educators already involved in cooperative education, the book has valuable suggestions for how to use the "defined-outcomes" methodology.

All two-year college administrators, counselors, and instructors; vocational and occupational specialists; and educational planners will find this book eminently useful—a thorough and completely practical sourcebook of facts and procedures.

"Dr. Heermann has put together principle and practice which draw on the best elements of vocational and the more general type of cooperative education"—*J. Dudley Dawson.*

THE AUTHOR

BARRY HEERMANN is associate professor and coordinator, marketing management programs, Sinclair Community Colleges, Dayton, Ohio.

JACKET DESIGN BY WILLI BAUM

JOSSEY-BASS PUBLISHERS
615 Montgomery Street, San Francisco 94111
3 Henrietta Street, London WC2E 8LU

LithoUSA1073

★★★★★★★★★★★★★★★★★★★★★★★★★★★★★★★★★★★★
★★★★★★★★★★★★★★★★★★★★★★★★★★★★★★★★★★★★

Cooperative Education in Community Colleges

A Sourcebook for
Occupational and General Educators

★★★★★★★★★★★★★★★★★★★★★★★★★★★★★★★★★★★★
★★★★★★★★★★★★★★★★★★★★★★★★★★★★★★★★★★★★

Barry Heermann

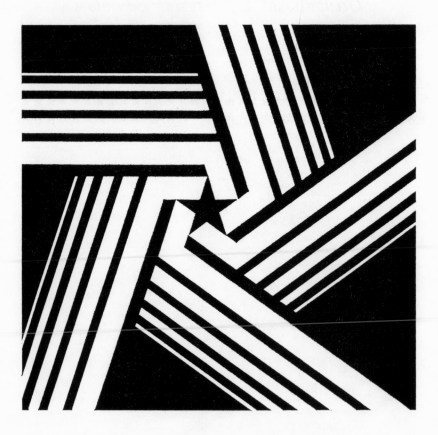

COOPERATIVE EDUCATION IN COMMUNITY COLLEGES

Jossey-Bass Publishers
San Francisco · Washington · London · 1973

COOPERATIVE EDUCATION IN COMMUNITY COLLEGES
A Sourcebook for Occupational and General Educators
by Barry Heermann

Copyright © 1973 by: Jossey-Bass, Inc., Publishers
615 Montgomery Street
San Francisco, California 94111

&

Jossey-Bass Limited
3 Henrietta Street
London WC2E 8LU

Library of Congress Catalogue Card Number LC 73-9072

International Standard Book Number ISBN 0-87589-195-0

Manufactured in the United States of America

JACKET DESIGN BY WILLI BAUM

FIRST EDITION

Code 7336

★★
★★

The Jossey-Bass Series
in Higher Education

★★
★★

Portions of this work were provided by

ERIC
Clearinghouse for Junior Colleges
University of California, Los Angeles

Arthur M. Cohen, *director*

*The ERIC (Educational Resources Information Center)
program is sponsored by the
United States Department of Health, Education, and Welfare,
National Institute of Education.
The points of view expressed here do not necessarily represent
official National Institute of Education position or policy.*

★★★★★★★★★★★★★★★★★★★★★★★★★★★★★★★★★★★★★★★
★★★★★★★★★★★★★★★★★★★★★★★★★★★★★★★★★★★★★★

Preface

★★★★★★★★★★★★★★★★★★★★★★★★★★★★★★★★★★★★★★★
★★★★★★★★★★★★★★★★★★★★★★★★★★★★★★★★★★★★★★

Cooperative education is winning widespread acceptance as an effective method of achieving educational objectives at both the college and the secondary levels. The classic *Cooperative Occupational Education* by Mason and Haines (1972) describes the cooperative vocational model widely practiced in high school programs all across the country; more recently, the *Handbook of Cooperative Education* (1971) by Asa Knowles and associates sets forth the philosophical and procedural dimensions at the collegiate level.

Cooperative Education in Community Colleges is designed to serve several purposes:

(1) To provide procedural guidelines for two-year college educators who administer or who are in the process of planning a cooperative education program;

(2) To serve as a sourcebook in courses in higher education, the community college, and vocational education, or in formal cooperative education courses designed to prepare students for careers in cooperative education coordination or administration; and

(3) To familiarize two-year college educators with the broad

purposes and operational dynamics of cooperative education in the community college.

One premise underlying the preparation of *Cooperative Education in Community Colleges* is that cooperative education ought to be fashioned to serve the specific educational mission of the community college, with its unique philosophical, functional, and organizational characteristics. To explore this theme, several of the country's exemplary programs are examined, and relevant literature on the subject is cited throughout the text. In Part One a model community college cooperative education program is presented. It is not expected that all readers will agree with all features of this model; I do hope that it will be thought-provoking, however, and that the procedural network presented will be useful to administrators who are interested in designing new programs or revising older ones.

Administrators in technical institutes, branch or extension campuses, junior colleges, or other two-year colleges should not be put off by the fact that most of my text references, for convenience, are to community colleges. Nor should general or university parallel educators conclude, because I advocate career education as an integral part of all college educational programs, that the book is only vocational or occupational in scope. It is not. In fact, one major contention of this book is that cooperative education has great applicability to the traditional liberal arts curriculum.

Community college cooperative educators have a clean slate. They may turn for ideas to the time-honored practices of secondary education on the one hand and to the experiences of the four-year colleges and universities on the other, but special focus needs to be given to the adaptation of cooperative education to the mission of community college education.

Cooperative Education in Community Colleges describes the special function of cooperative education in the community college setting, and outlines procedures that could be used by administrators in operating such a program. The book has three major divisions. Part One traces the development of cooperative education and its associated philosophies, offers a model for a comprehensive cooperative education program, and examines program potentials and possible pitfalls. Part Two sets forth planning and organizational guidelines, and Part Three explains numerous operational subtleties that are crucial to an effective program, including the important "defined-outcomes" methodology. Specifically, the book examines the philosophies of vocational and general cooperative education, the community college institutional setting, the applicability of defined outcomes, the role of the employer, instructor, and coordinator, the selection and development of employers, organizational alternatives, promotion of the program, guidance activities, evaluation and feedback, and other topics critical to the administration of community college cooperative education.

Acknowledgements for advice and suggestions useful in the preparation of this material go to Robert Custis, James Puthoff, and Ned Sifferlen of Sinclair Community College in Ohio; to Vaughn Redding, Director of the Coast Community College cooperative education program in California; to Harry Heinemann and Sheila Gordon, Dean and Assistant Dean of the mandatory cooperative education program at La Guardia Community College in New York; to Edward Lewis, Dean of the Cooperative Education Program at the Borough of Manhattan Community College and past president of the Cooperative Education Association, and to his coordinators Harriet Van Sickle and Iolani Miller; to Clifford House, President of Cincinnati Technical College; to Neal Vivian, Teacher-Educator, Ohio State University; to the friendly and helpful staff members of the Vocational Technical ERIC Clearinghouse and the Junior College ERIC Clearinghouse; and to cooperative education administrators too numerous to list here. Special thanks for reviewing the manuscript and offering useful suggestions go to J. Dudley Dawson, Vice President and Dean of Students Emeritus, Antioch College, and Consultant for the National Commission on Cooperative Education and currently consultant to Sinclair and several other community colleges; to Robert Bennett, project director of the California Community College Cooperative Education Consortium; to Edward Ferguson, Research and Development Specialist at the Center for Vocational and Technical Education, Ohio State University; to John Lombardi, former President of Los Angeles City College and Assistant Superintendent of Los Angeles Community Colleges; and to Arthur M. Cohen, Director of the ERIC Clearinghouse for Junior Colleges, who gave me great encouragement in preparing the material for the book. Thanks also to my wife Pat Heermann, who accompanied me on visits to exemplary programs, made suggestions about the development of the manuscript, and laboriously typed early drafts of the text.

I dedicate this book to Carl Becker, Robert Johnson, and to my parents.

Dayton, Ohio   BARRY HEERMANN
September 1973

Contents

xiii

★★★★★★★★★★★★★★★★★★★★★★★★★★★★★★★★★★★★★★★
★★★★★★★★★★★★★★★★★★★★★★★★★★★★★★★★★★★★★★★

Cooperative Education in Community Colleges

A Sourcebook for
Occupational and General Educators

★★★★★★★★★★★★★★★★★★★★★★★★★★★★★★★★★★★★★★★
★★★★★★★★★★★★★★★★★★★★★★★★★★★★★★★★★★★★★★★

★★★★★★★★★★★★★ 1 ★★★★★★★★★★★★★
★★★★★★★★★★★★★   ★★★★★★★★★★★★★

A Framework
for Cooperative
Education

★★★★★★★★★★★★★★★★★★★★★★★★★★★★★★★★★★★★
★★★★★★★★★★★★★★★★★★★★★★★★★★★★★★★★★★★★

The community college can be usefully viewed as an extension of the community—an institution whose very existence is dependent upon the community and whose justification is the service of the educational needs of its populace. The "ivory tower" notion of separation of college and community to preserve educational integrity and purpose is disclaimed. In its place is the philosophical stance that the college ought to be integrated with the community and its vital economic and social pursuits: "The term [community college] connotes a close interrelationship of the college and the life of the community; the college looks to the community for suggestions in program planning and the community looks to the college for many different services to many people" (Medsker, 1960, p. 6).

Those community colleges that best maintain the integrity of their mission use mechanisms for facilitating community inputs,

1

coupled with carefully conceived feedback systems: community surveys; participation by the college staff in community, professional, and social service organizations; placement of the campus in the heart of the urban core; and an active advisory committee structure. But is it enough? Does the theoretical and philosophical construct for *community* college coincide with the reality of its function and operation? Can the institution really be kept "honest" in its commitment to purpose? The thesis of this book is that the single best hope of achieving the community aspect of the community college philosophy is a carefully planned and organized comprehensive cooperative education program.

As the numerous attempts at definition and evaluation (for instance, Thornton, 1966; Blocker, Plummer, and Richardson, 1965; Cohen, 1969, 1971; Cohen and Brawer, 1972) suggest, the community college is an intricate patchwork of functions and images. While there is certainly a lack of consensus about what the community junior college is, or what it should be, certain parameters nevertheless are important to community college cooperative education. First, community colleges have a multiplicity of functions; that is, the community college typically provides an elaborate array of occupational programs in addition to a program of general education. Developmental programs in reading, mathematics, and English assist students in preparing for college-level work, and university parallel programs are provided for those who want to continue on for the bachelor's degree. Evening school and Saturday college programs cater to full-time employees returning to college for upgrading or retraining programs. In short, the community college provides service to an amazingly broad spectrum of community needs.

Cooperative education can be adapted to the varied educational missions of the community college. Of particular significance, it offers the potential for a rejuvenation of the community dimension of the community college. This new potential for community is the direct result of the college's active participation in the community's economic, social, and technological activity. Its implications for the college go far beyond the development of curriculum based upon community survey or advisory committee advice. They go beyond providing cultural programs, "things-to-do" projects, or social services. The concept of community advocated here provides a thoroughgoing merger of college resources with community resources. Consider the possibility of students trained in disciplines related to community occupational needs and placed in hospitals, commercial enterprises, engineering laboratories, social agencies, schools, and industrial firms as an integral part of their education—a program creating a partnership between and uniting college and community.

Cooperative education has gained wide acceptance at the secondary levels, usually in vocational education programs; at the university and the four-year college, in professional as well as liberal arts programs; and, of course, more recently in community and other two-year colleges. Support for cooperative education comes from many levels. President Lyndon Johnson, in his 1967 educational message to Congress, spoke of the success of cooperative education in integrating work and study and called for a wider application of it in the nation's schools and universities (Probst, 1971, p. 322). And community college authority B. Lamar Johnson (1969, p. 68) calls cooperative education one of the ten most significant innovations in community college education. But what precisely is cooperative education? According to James Wilson (1970, pp. 2–8), "the introduction into the curriculum of a different kind of experience . . . is the defining characteristic, the essence of cooperative education." That "different kind of experience," he concludes, can best be termed "nonscholastic work" rather than the traditional "employment," which suggests a preoccupation with wages and not education (see also Hatcher, 1969, p. 1). Cooperative education, then, is "a strategy of nonscholastic work incorporated into the curriculum and carried out by students, the object of which is to assist students to meet those developmental goals appropriate to their age level."

A theme central to this book is that cooperative education at the community college should be interpreted to include the notion of *comprehensiveness*. That is, because of the unique philosophy of the community college and its permutation of functions, cooperative education should not be considered relevant to only one or a few programs but should be available in all of the diverse programs for community college students. The notion that cooperative education should be limited to particular program areas (e.g. as an adjunct to vocational curriculums) needs rejecting so that its important impact to the breadth of community college education can begin to be understood (See Chapter Two)'.

Historical Sketch

Cooperative education is not a recent educational contrivance. The roots of this movement can be traced back to the earliest civilizations (see in particular Roberts, 1965, pp. 31–112). At the beginning of the twentieth century important cooperative education developments came about at the collegiate level, the most notable development taking place at the University of Cincinnati. In 1906 Herman Schneider of the university's school of engineering observed that many facets of engineering cannot be learned in the classroom but only through direct on-the-job experience with professionals already successful in the field. He also observed that the part-time jobs that many students seek have no relationship to their ultimate career choices and therefore do not contribute to their professional education (Wooldridge, 1964, pp. 11–16). These observations led Professor Schneider to establish the country's first program of collegiate cooperative education, at the University of Cincinnati. The first liberal arts college to provide a program of cooperative education was Antioch College in 1921, under the leadership of Arthur Morgan (Auld, 1971, p. 8). During this same period the first two-year colleges, most of which were technical institutes, adopted cooperative programs (see Barbeau, 1972)'. The movement at this level was begun by Rochester Athenæum and the Mechanics Institute in New York in 1912. The Ohio College of Applied Science and Wyomissing Polytechnic Institute in Pennsylvania followed with two-year cooperative technical programs. These curriculums were predominantly engineering.

Riverside Junior College in California was the first junior college to adopt cooperative education (1922)'; it offered cooperative education as an option in nursing, library science, architecture, engineering, and other vocational areas. In 1928 at Marin Junior College a work-study program was initiated in conjunction with banks, steamship companies, and railroads in San Francisco (Eells,

1931, pp. 306–307). In 1924 Garland Junior College in Boston offered its own cooperative program, and by 1939 fourteen junior colleges had programs (Barbeau, 1972, p. 99). There were forty-one programs in 1941 (Eells, 1931, p. 171).

Examination of the Cooperative Education Association roster for 1973 reveals that over 350 cooperative education programs are in operation at the collegiate level. Of this number approximately 40 percent are two-year college programs. However, many other two-year colleges offer cooperative education but do not file with the major cooperative education organizations. For instance, many two-year colleges not accounted for in the statistics are operating vocationally funded programs under the 1968 Vocational Amendments and have professional affiliation with the American Vocational Association. Wilson's 1972 survey of cooperative education in higher education included seventy-six two-year colleges. His survey findings give some notion of the scope of cooperative education programs in community colleges. Approximately two thirds of these programs were begun between 1961 and 1970; and more than one fourth were begun between 1971 and 1972, demonstrating the youthfulness of most programs.

Associations of Cooperative Educators

Collegiate cooperative education associations can be traced back to an organization assembled in 1926 under the direction of Herman Schneider at the University of Cincinnati. Soon thereafter the Cooperative Education Division of the American Society of Engineering Education was formed and became the medium of exchange among educators and employers engaged in cooperative education—most of whom were in engineering schools or in industrial organizations. This organization is still active.

Various affiliations of secondary education and two-year college educators at the state and national level, through the American Vocational Association, provided a focus on cooperative vocational education. This association, through its leadership and its sponsorship of legislation for vocational education, has provided much of the impetus for cooperative education programs in high schools, technical institutes, and junior and community colleges.

In 1962 the National Commission for Cooperative Education was organized through an initial grant of the Charles F. Kettering Foundation. Prior to the creation of this commission, Kettering, a long-time research director of General Motors and a strong advocate of cooperative education, had sponsored several national conferences on cooperative education, which led to an important research study supported by the Fund for the Advancement of Cooperative Education (Wilson and Lyons, 1961).

The Cooperative Education Association (CEA) was founded in 1963 to provide a comprehensive range of membership, including colleges, employers, and others interested in cooperative education. The annual meeting of the CEA is combined with the Cooperative Education Division of the American Society of Engineering Education (CED) to provide information and interchange between two- and four-year colleges and universities and educators and employers representing almost every field of study and human endeavor.

Conferences on cooperative education in the two-year college are held throughout the country. One such association of community college educators is the "Florida experiment in higher education" whereby the University of South Florida has actively encouraged community college interest in cooperative education by providing an advisory service and the sponsorship of a state-wide junior college conference. The first conference, held in October 1968, was attended by more than two thirds of the public community colleges in that state. The university not only sponsored the conference but established a plan whereby a transferring two-year college student can transfer cooperative education credits to a Florida university. Several programs were initiated as a result of the conference; a notable exemplary program is that of the Miami-Dade Junior College South Campus, which was operationalized in partnership with the University of South Florida (Lupton and Wadsworth, 1969, pp. 50–57).

Wilson (in Knowles, 1971, pp. 16–17) has made these comments concerning Florida community colleges: "By far the most dramatic growth is occurring in Florida, where nearly twenty junior colleges have initiated programs within the past two years and where the State University System of Florida has adopted a policy of implementing programs of cooperative education on every college campus in Florida. The cooperative plan has been viewed by community colleges as particularly appropriate, because they all have career-related curricula which can be greatly strengthened by a policy of off-campus work and because the cooperative plan helps to relate the college and the community much more closely."

California community colleges have responded with remarkable commitment to the philosophy of cooperative education under the dynamism of the five-college consortium of cooperative education community colleges with project leadership from San Mateo college district. This consortium, in concert with other community colleges, meets periodically in special conferences to review the peculiar operational problems of community college cooperative education in that state. In California and all across the country, community college cooperative educators are meeting in short conferences; this kind of interchange may in the future foster a new association specifically geared to cooperative education in two-year colleges. The Conference of California Community Colleges (held February 24–26, 1972, at the Disneyland Hotel) and the Western Regional Cooperation Education Conference (conducted November 27–28, 1972, in San Francisco) are illustrative of the vitality of cooperative education in the West.

Federal Funding of Cooperative Education

In 1968 federal funding of cooperative education was ensured when Congress approved certain amendments to the Vocational Education Act of 1963. Funds available under the Vocational Amendments (Parts B and G for existing and developing programs) were provided for cooperative vocational education in high schools and two-year colleges. These vocational funds are administered through the states and their respective educational agencies as provided by a carefully developed state plan. Under the Vocational Amendments Act, Part G, the following funds were appropriated for use by high schools, vocational schools, two-year colleges, and technical institutes: $14,000,000 in 1970–1971, $18,500,000 in 1971–1972, and $19,500,000 for 1972–1973 (*Education Daily,* Aug. 4, 1972, p. 5). In addition, Congress amended the Higher Education Act of 1965 to provide funds for grants to assist institutions of higher education (two- and four-year college and universities) in developing new programs of cooperative education or strengthening existing ones. The federal government made appropriations of $1,500,000 for use in 1970–1971, $1,600,000 in 1971–1972, and $1,700,000 for 1972–1973 for cooperative education grants. The laws authorizing expenditures for cooperative education were extended by new legislation in 1972 covering the years 1973–1974, 1974–1975, and 1975–1976. It should be pointed out that federal funding covers only partial support for those programs qualifying under the established guidelines of the Division of College Support, Bureau of Higher Education, U.S. Office of Education. Furthermore, applicants for program administration are limited to $75,000 and three one-year grants. Support is also available under the same act for training programs and research in cooperative education. In the long run, cooperative education must be regarded as a regularly budgeted item in the college program.

Community College Cooperative Education: Ready for Launch

Cooperative education holds great promise for the fulfillment of the community college mission in higher education. The relevance of this educational formula—called variously experiential learning, cooperative education, or work-experience education—should be of particular significance to community college educators, given their special institutional purpose. The groundwork has been laid as cooperative educators in two-year colleges move from the pioneering stage of its development to a period of extensive expansion. Its rich historical past, its developing structure of professional associations, and the recent stimulus of federal government support establishes a clearly bright and prosperous future for cooperative education.

Robert Bennett, project director for the California Community College Cooperative Education Consortium program, predicts that 25 percent of all California students will be enrolled in cooperative education programs by the early 1980s (1971, p. 4). Wilson (1971, pp. 790–794) envisions a significantly broadened role for cooperative education in the community college: "The brightest future for cooperative education appears to lie with the community colleges and technical institutes. Their growth in American higher education borders on the phenomenal. . . . by 1980 junior colleges will constitute a much larger proportion, even the major proportion, of higher institutions' operating programs of cooperative education."

From Herman Schneider at the University of Cincinnati, to Arthur Morgan at Antioch, to Riverside Junior College, to its present expansion at the community college, cooperative education can boast a rich tradition and a demonstrably effective service for the needs of students. The community college–cooperative education amalgamation is a significant development that has the potential for making an important new contribution to community growth and development. Chapter Two presents one possible direction that community college educators might take in the creation of a new model: a *comprehensive* cooperative education model evolved for the specific institutional setting of the community college.

Cooperative Education Dichotomy

In contrast to the high school, with its practice of cooperative vocational education, and the four-year college or university, with its diversified pattern of cooperative education in professional career areas or the liberal arts, community college cooperative educators have no clear model or established tradition of cooperative education operation. There is evidence that a particular brand of institutional cooperative education philosophy may be "lifted" without sufficient thought to its relationship to institutional mission. That is, there is a clear danger that meeting community need and designing cooperative education to conform to college philosophy may become secondary to launching a program—any cooperative program. The proverbial "tail wagging the dog" incongruity is indeed a threat, as some community college educators can eagerly "jump on the bandwagon" without concern for the subtleties of cooperative education variation and orientation.

A sampling of community college cooperative education programs reveals that some are patterned precisely after the vocational educational model widely used at the secondary level, with a highly

Table 1

CHARACTERISTICS OF TWO COOPERATIVE EDUCATION MODELS

Characteristic	Vocational Education Model	General Education Model
Institutional Practice	Many high school programs operate under this formula as do some community colleges and most technical institutes.	Numerous colleges (two- and four-year) and universities (including preprofessional, professional, and graduate programs) operate under this formula.
Program Objective	To foster technical and conceptual skill development in an area of occupational specialization in order to prepare students to accept positions of responsibility in the world of work.	To stimulate the student's intellectual career and personal development in response to a wide range of student needs.
Coordinator Function	To coordinate job training in the area of the student's career objective with correlated classroom studies designed to foster vocational skill development.	To provide a variety of work experiences in response to student's educational needs (personal, career, or intellectual).
Organizational Placement	Coordination is decentralized by combining the function of coordinator and vocational instructor in high schools and some two-year college programs, but a centralized staff department frequently provides for the co-op service in two-year collegiate programs.	A centralized department provides co-op services in most four-year and many two-year colleges—occasionally with liaison or part-time participation of faculty.
Federal Funding	Matching state and federal monies created through vocational education legislation (i.e., nonbaccalaureate programs).	Funded through the Higher Education Act.
Work-Study Sequence	Students typically alternate study and work periods on a half-day or term (quarter or semester) basis.	Students typically alternate work and study each quarter or semester in these programs but may carry study and work schedules concurrently with reduced work and study loads.

structured and specialized career program rigidly directed at the development of an occupational skill (Mason and Haines, 1972). Others, fewer in number, have adopted what might be referred to as the Antioch model (Dixon and Bush, 1966) whereby personal development and exploration, including career exploration, are stressed. Specific occupational skill development is not a major thrust of this cooperative philosophy, which emphasizes exploration of a range of experiences. Both cooperative education styles are entirely valid to the degree that they conform with the college's philosophy in meeting student needs. But the question that must be posed is this: is the decision to practice a particular co-op style conditioned on identifiable student needs and institutional missions or on an uncritical adaptation of a style of cooperative education that a university or secondary program has had success with? Table 1 shows the basic dichotomous elements found in varying degrees in secondary, two-year, senior college, and university cooperative programs. These are theoretical constructs designed to foster understanding of the breadth of cooperative education modes; in reality these forms may be practiced in combination and with varying states of embellishment.

Dawson (1972, pp. 1–3) comments on the varying styles of cooperative education competing for community college loyalties: "The concept and operation of cooperative education in community colleges is unfortunately clouded and confused by two differing philosophies of education, one bearing the name of 'vocational cooperative education' and the other more general type usually named 'general cooperative education.' " Vocational cooperative education is governed and funded through the Bureau of Vocational Education in the United States Office of Education; general cooperative education is governed and funded by the Bureau of Higher Education. According to the Bureau of Vocational Education (as cited by Dawson, 1971, pp. 5–6) "Cooperative vocational education is an interdependent combination of vocational instruction and employment. . . . Employment under this arrangement is conceived to be an extension of in-school instruction. . . . A cooperative vocational education program, therefore, is designed to serve an educational or training objective. Students participate in a cooperative program because they wish to acquire qualifications for a predetermined area of competitive employment." In contrast, the general type of cooperative education provides elements of self-development best achieved through experience; explores occupational interests and skills as a means for making or confirming a career choice or directing further education; helps the student attain basic vocational or preprofessional preparation; and utilizes work experience as a means of supplementary classroom learning in both general and specialized education.

Mason and Haines (1972, pp. 19, 21) distinguish between cooperative education (which is viewed as a distinctly vocational method) and work experience (which is seen as general education):

> *There is . . . among some groups of Amercian educators an unfortunate degree of confusion about the difference between cooperative education and work-experience education. In some cases the confusion has been due to the surface resemblance of the programs. . . . In other cases confusion has arisen from poorly operated cooperative programs—ones which turned out to be just "plain work experience" through such errors as inadequate supervision, lack of correlated classroom instruction, and the enrollment of any student without qualification. . . . General work experience can be successful in its general objectives of retaining youth . . . and giving exploratory experiences; but it is quite improbable that general work-experience programs can develop occupational competence. Developing job competence following career objectives of students is the task of cooperative occupational education.*

Biester (1970, pp. 53–54), speaking on behalf of the liberal education model, points out that cooperative education "began as an adjunct to engineering education and it stayed that way for most of the early years, with other technical or technological curricula slowly discovering its advantages and benefits. Even today many co-op administrators reject any other arrangement. . . . The major problem has been that traditional co-op programs are too narrow in their philosophy and implementation to serve the needs of diverse student bodies." Similarly, Dubé (1971, p. 18) suggests that cooperative education has been limited by its traditional conception as a "purely occupational education endeavor."

A survey of over one hundred collegiate cooperative education program (Chase, 1971, pp. 49–52) reveals that the primary objective of their cooperative efforts is "career development." (The reader should be guarded in the interpretation of this finding, because some define career development broadly to include marriage, family, and citizenship, as well as work.) The liberal arts or general cooperative education aim of "personal development" is second to the primary program goal. Wilson's 1972 study of 243 cooperative colleges, 76 of which were two-year colleges, reveals that 80 percent of the two-year colleges see "career development" as their principal objective and 88 percent seek work experiences directly related to the student's discipline of study.

Dawson (1972, p. 3) calls for a "different and more flexible meaning" for career education, arguing that the traditionally stringent structuring of a program to a narrow field needs to be reexamined. The more flexible meaning that he advocates would allow for exploration of career interests for students uncertain about careers, work experience designed to meet educational needs not necessarily identified with a specified career, and stress on "personal development and the strengthening of the general as well as the specialized aspects of the student's educational program."

Ingram (1956, p. 1), a past president of the American Vocational Association, speaks out vociferously for the values of vocational education: "In the sense that education is preparation for and adjustment to life, and work is a major factor in everyone's life, all education can be thought of as vocational preparation in a very broad, general sense. . . . Vocational education has [however] come to be accepted as that phase of education designed to improve the proficiency of an individual for and/or in a specific occupation."

Venn (1964, p. 1) has mandated, "All levels of education, *and particularly postsecondary education*, must move quickly to assume greater responsibility for preparing men and women for entry into the changed and changing world of technological work." But what form of preparation will best serve that end? Is cooperative education so narrowly conceived as to restrict total development of the student? Is it practical to assume that general cooperative education can accomplish for many students the same occupational preparation as cooperative vocational education? Is it necessary that community college educators choose between one of two cooperative ideologies? Is it logical to assume that students' needs are so homogeneous as to be satisfied by a single cooperative education style? Is it possible for both cooperative education styles to coexist in the same institution?

Philosophies of education impinge upon the orientation of cooperative education, and it is critically important for community college educators to guard against the mistaken notion that cooperative education is a single, nondifferentiated program with one central mission. This is simply not the case. Cooperative education can be shaped and structured to fit particular missions whether it be career exploration, personal development, upgrading, career preparation, or programs serving the disadvantaged. The burden of decision rests with the community college administrator, who in reality has options beyond one of two cooperative education styles. Educators in the community college must evolve a new vision of cooperative education in light of their numerous and varied missions premised on service to a diversity of student needs. A multifaceted cooperative education system with the capability of adapting to a whole range of student orientations is clearly needed. Chapter Two suggests one possible structure—a comprehensive cooperative education model designed to a community college specification.

★★★★★★★★★★★★★★ 2 ★★★★★★★★★★★★★★
★★★★★★★★★★★★★★   ★★★★★★★★★★★★★★

A Formula
for Cooperative
Education

★★
★★

Presenting new formulas for community college education is an activity engaged in by increasing numbers of educators. Everyone is in on the act. The *Community and Junior College Journal* is replete with articles on programmed instruction, developmental education, new organizational strategies, or the latest vocational program innovation. These new formulas are typically subsystems having specific tactical implications to the mission of the institution (the most notable exception is the sweeping and pervasive recommendation for a model community college by Arthur M. Cohen in *Dateline '79,* which was clearly strategical in its conception). A thesis of this book is that cooperative education's contribution will be significantly limited should community college administrators see it "tactically," as just another interesting innovation which "perhaps our college can find *some* application for *somewhere* in *some* program." Cooperative education is strategic to the fulfillment of the community thrust of community college.

As those community colleges with vital and thriving programs have evidenced, commitment is essential to the success of cooperative education programs. Administrations committed to the values provided by experiential learning have secured program success in no more mystifying ways than community college administrators have secured program success in a student services program or in instructional endeavors. But a cooperative education program must be undertaken only after a reexamination of community college philosophy, objectives, organization, and function— especially if the program is to achieve a strategic role in reaching institutional objectives. Viewing it tactically may be rationalized as a "safer" or lower-risk posture administratively, but this position serves only to cloud its possible contributions to student growth. The question ought not to be "Will it work?" but "What level of administrative action is essential to program success?" Cooperative education can and does work if administrative commitment is up to the task.

Phase 1: Foundations

In this chapter a model cooperative education program will be set forth as a part of a total community college strategy. The model is structured on a set of premises about cooperative education in the community college. The first premise is that cooperative education offers unusual value to students, employers, college, and community alike. A discussion of those values is presented in the next chapter.

A second premise is that cooperative education should be integrated in all program areas. The view that cooperative education is the exclusive domain of vocational education and somehow is not relevant to other student needs is myopic and substantially debilitates its possible contribution. Comprehensive community colleges ought to provide for comprehensive cooperative education. Programs for the disadvantaged, career preparation, liberal arts, career search, evening programs, and the whole maze of community college endeavors should be programmed with cooperative education. In addition, given certain prerequisites—an adequate employment base, sufficient resources, and institutional commitment—the program should be mandatory (in the tradition of La Guardia Community College or Cincinnati Technical College) so that all students have the advantage of experiential learning. Cooperative education can provide a significant stimulus to the realization of a viable community orientation actively fulfilling the community aspect of community college.

The third premise is based upon the demonstrably valuable defined-outcome approach (Cohen, 1969). That is, the college should specify the behavioral changes sought via classroom instruction and during work-experience periods (procedural aspects are presented in Chapter Eight); these objectives are termed *micro defined outcomes*. In addition, the model provides for *macro objectives*, or a statement by the college of the kinds of outcomes students can expect as a result of successful completion of the total program. The thrust of this approach is that colleges need to be responsible for their graduates (see Venn, 1967). Although the college cannot, of course, guarantee a job or a transfer to a university, it can and should clearly indicate the kinds of opportunities available upon graduation. An effort at defining macro outcomes can help keep the institution honest in serving student needs.

The fourth and final premise, closely related to the third, is that community colleges need to refine and sharpen a student (rather than a process) orientation. Consider the bewilderment of a new student enrolling at the community college; much of what he first confronts—a maze of curricula, course offerings, and course descriptions—is unintelligible to him. The two years of study are part of some mysterious ceremony performed because of values which are all too often obscure. A better life will miraculously result from this experience, he is told. His own needs and objectives, if they have been contemplated at all, are only indirectly related to the educational experience. The community college cooperative education program to be presented attempts to provide a strengthened student orientation by a careful presentation of options and their associated outcomes at the time of admission and on an ongoing basis without belaboring individual course requirements and other process subtleties. The value of cooperative education—the blending of work and study—is outlined for the student for each of several broad program areas. In the paragraphs to follow, these premises will be elaborated upon in conjunction with a presentation of some procedural guidelines (rationale and further operational details will be discussed in later chapters).

The model program presented in this chapter shall be referred to as a comprehensive cooperative education community college. Such a college provides an education that is markedly different in three important ways: the educational experience emphasizes a blending of in-class theoretical constructs with real-world community involvement in business, engineering, health occupations, or one of a number of human service areas; the educational experience is specifically related to broad areas of need, as expressed by most students, and not simply to networks of course descriptions; finally, the college commits itself, in as specific a way as possible, to a sequence of particular outcomes that students might expect upon graduation.

Upon admission, the student is intensively tested to determine deficiencies in basic-skill areas, so that the college can intelligently advise him of desirable developmental courses. A second purpose of testing is to determine educational and vocational interests and aptitudes of the newly admitted student so as to assist him in selecting the right program niche. This very critical decision as to program niche is all too frequently assumed to come about via the student's careful decoding of the college bulletin and perhaps an initial meeting with a counselor or an academic advisor. Some community colleges require that this decision be made prior to the student's first contacts with college personnel. The mere ability to interpret the jigsaw puzzle called "college bulletin" might well be sufficient to award the student some credit toward his degree. It is made all the more complicated by the addition of a comprehensive cooperative education program.

The model cooperative education community college presented here offers a differentiated set of work and study programs, each gauged to satisfy a particular student need. A list of frequently mentioned student needs is given to the student, and he is asked to match his own predisposition toward life, education, and work with the need-satisfying qualities of each program. Identification of a student's educational requirements or needs is followed by the college's commitment to an outcome of rather specific service to the student's ambition. This statement of defined outcome (macro) is premised upon certain conditions and performance levels the student must demonstrate.

The broad program services or educational processes, it is explained to the student, are called "coopportunity clusters"—for two reasons: (1) that nomenclature stresses the opportunity the college's educational process can provide; (2) it suggests the cooperative education thrust of the program, whereby the student's progress toward his goals is met by a merging of traditional in-class instruction with experiential learning. That is, the student begins practicing, testing, and critically evaluating his own needs in a real-world laboratory. The cooperative education community college model would preserve the flexibility to provide a multifaceted educational service suggested by the comprehensive community college philosophy, which emphasizes open admissions, strong student orientation, heavy guidance emphasis, close student-instructor relationships, comprehensive curriculum transfer, adult-evening, occupational, developmental, and a strong community service bias.

Since a comprehensive curriculum designed to meet a whole range of student needs is a hallmark of the comprehensive community college philosophy, the proposed community college model establishes a mandate for *comprehensive* cooperative education. In pursuit of this mission, cooperative education in the envisioned community college is not viewed as the exclusive property of one department or splinter of the college's educational program; with certain minimal changes in orientation, objectives, and requirements for student reports, work experience can be geared to any of a range of student needs, from vocational-skill preparation to career search to a broadly defined personal development program. In addition, this cooperative education model embellishes all programs with a career orientation. Career exploration is no longer exclusively the domain of occupational educators. Instead, all students take part in career education, albeit a new notion of career education. The comprehensive cooperative education community college model broadens the definition of career education to include more than the traditional vocational areas, such as distributive education, technical and industrial education, or business education, wherein students alternate periods of specialized technical study with work experience directly related to their career objective. This option is still preserved and carefully nurtured in the proposed community college, but experience in business or the social services is now integrated in all programs as career education achieves new stature and students are enrolled in career-education courses prior to their work experience and concurrently with each work period. Career consciousness becomes a reality in this model community college program.

The ivory-tower notion of college as a closed society is discarded. In business, education, engineering, social welfare, public services, and cultural activities, the community and the college are bound together in a new partnership. Students are actively involved in the affairs of the community at all levels, and the demarcation between the college and the community becomes increasingly blurred. The *community* college becomes a viable and explicitly fulfilling concept.

As for program and curriculum format, students would be asked to choose from the following clusters: (A) Occupational, Commitment; (B) Occupational, Exploration; (C) Occupational, Professional Orientation; (D) Occupational, Advancement; (E) Personal Development, Intellectual Exploration; (F) Personal Development, Goals Identification; (G) Personal Development, Basic Skills. After meetings with college guidance personnel (to review previous study and work record, test scores, and personal and career objectives) and after selecting a cluster, the student is assigned an advisor in the area of his particular interest.

Figures 1 through 7 show the various program clusters. This description of important program characteristics would be presented to the student in a special student handbook at the time of his admission. For each program cluster a student frame of reference is presented; these points of reference express typical needs of entering community college students. The student is asked to match his needs to the statement which most nearly coincides with his own educational requirements. There is also a cluster for students who do not have well-conceived educational objectives (cluster F).

(*text continued on page 27*)

Figure 1. PROGRAM CLUSTER A: Occupational, Commitment

STUDENT FRAME OF REFERENCE:

I have a clearly defined career objective in a middle-management, technical, or semiprofessional occupational area [retail store buyer, mental health technician, engineering draftsman, etc.] and desire a skill-oriented, vocational program which would permit entry into this occupational specialization after graduation.

PROGRAM OUTCOME:

Student will develop work skills necessary to secure employment in a selected technical, semiprofessional, or middle-management category of work.

Student will successfully complete an associate degree program, of a minimum of two years duration, alternating periods of specialized career instruction at the college with work directly related to career orientation.

Student will demonstrate the development of specialized social, technical, and conceptual skills critical to his employment objective.

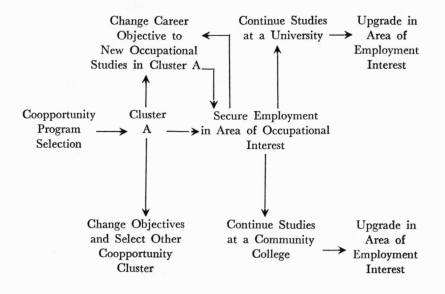

Figure 2. PROGRAM CLUSTER B: Occupational, Exploration

STUDENT FRAME OF REFERENCE:

I want to go to work after graduation in a semiprofessional, middle-management, or technical occupational position, but I have not decided on a particular occupational area.

PROGRAM OUTCOME:

Student will develop work skills necessary to secure employment in a selected technical, semiprofessional or middle-management category.

Student will successfully complete an associate degree program, of a minimum of two and a half years duration, receiving special vocational guidance, varied work experiences, and a career-exploration curriculum core leading to a specialized work and study component as he narrows his career choice.

Student will demonstrate the development of specialized social, technical, and conceptual skills critical to his employment objective.

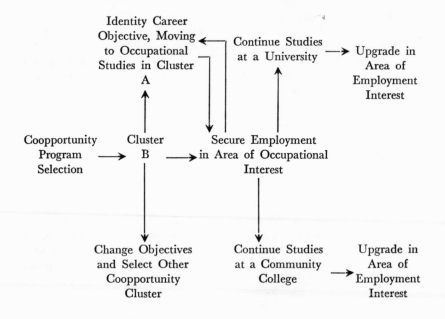

Figure 3. PROGRAM CLUSTER C: Occupational,
Professional Orientation

STUDENT FRAME OF REFERENCE:

I have a well-defined career objective which embraces a professional occupational responsibility (medical doctor, lawyer, engineer, teacher, etc.) and which I am aware requires the completion of a bachelor's degree or special graduate degree programs.

PROGRAM OUTCOME:

Student will be prepared to transfer to a university or college which provides professional training in his career area.

Student will successfully complete an associate degree program, of a minimum of two years duration, wherein he will study social science, humanities, and science areas with some technical subjects related to the area of professional interest on an alternating basis with work experience related to his long-range career goals.

Student will demonstrate the development of specialized social, technical, and conceptual skills critical to his employment objective.

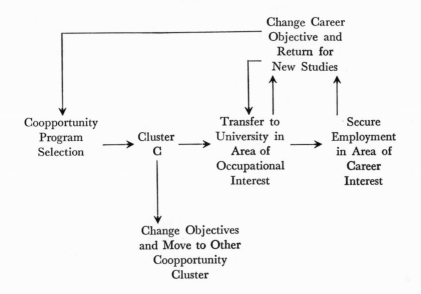

Figure 4.   Program Cluster D: Occupational, Advancement

STUDENT FRAME OF REFERENCE:

I am presently employed full time and desire upgrading or advancement in my area of occupational interest through a skill-oriented vocational program of study.

PROGRAM OUTCOME:

Student will develop skills necessary to accept increased responsibility and commensurate advancement in his area of occupational interest.

Student will successfully complete a certificate or associate degree program, of a minimum of two years or three and a half years, wherein he completes specialized career instruction in conjunction with a specially arranged employment sequence with his employer.

Student will demonstrate the development of specialized social, technical, and conceptual skills critical to his employment objective.

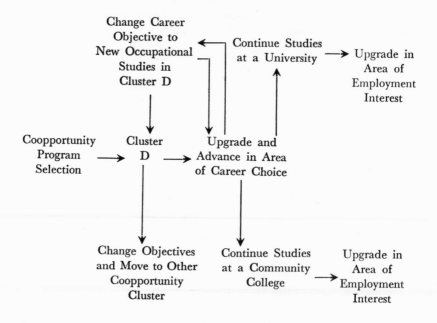

Figure 5.   PROGRAM CLUSTER E: Personal Development,
Intellectual Exploration

STUDENT FRAME OF REFERENCE:

I am not presently interested in development of skills for occupational en-
trance but desire to explore science, humanities, and social science areas
for personal fulfillment and perhaps transfer later to a university for continued exploration or professional studies.

PROGRAM OUTCOME:

Student will satisfactorily complete an interdisciplinary program of study,
critical to an understanding of man and his environment and useful to personal direction, enlightment, growth, and maturity.

Student will successfully complete an associate degree program, of a minimum of two years duration, alternating periods of general education studies
at the college with a variety of work experience in business and the human
services.

Student will demonstrate the development of specialized social, technical, and
conceptual skills critical to his personal growth and maturity.

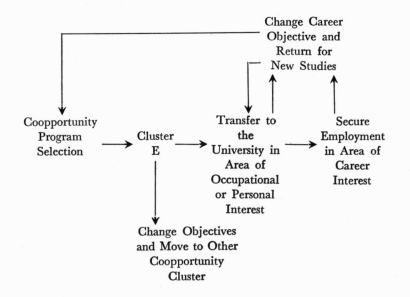

Figure 6.   PROGRAM CLUSTER F: Personal Development,
Goals Identification

STUDENT FRAME OF REFERENCE:

I have not yet clearly identified my educational, personal, and career objectives and desire counseling and a program of study whereby I can carefully examine my interests and relationships with my surroundings in order to chart new directions.

PROGRAM OUTCOME:

Student will satisfactorily complete an interdisciplinary program of study, including a survey of occupational opportunities and a special guidance program.

Student will successfully complete an associate degree program, of a minimum of two years duration, alternating periods of general education studies at the college with a variety of work experience in business and/or human services (with the option of changing to coopportunity clusters A, B, C, or E.)

Student will demonstrate the development of specialized social, technical, and conceptual skills critical to his personal growth and development.

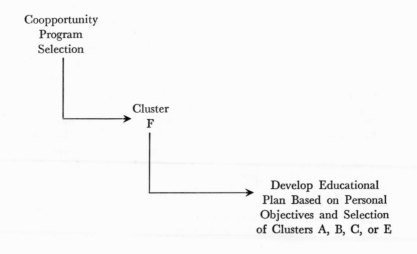

Coopportunity
Program
Selection

Cluster
F

Develop Educational
Plan Based on Personal
Objectives and Selection
of Clusters A, B, C, or E

Figure 7. PROGRAM CLUSTER G: Personal Development, Basic Skills

STUDENT FRAME OF REFERENCE:

I desire development of basic skills in mathematics and communications before selecting coopportunity clusters A through F.

PROGRAM OUTCOME:

Student will satisfactorily perform basic mathematics and communication operations.

Student will successfully complete a sequence of basic-skill courses over one to four quarters in alternation with work experience in his selected area of interest.

Student will demonstrate basic-skills proficiency prerequisite to entry in coopportunity clusters A through F.

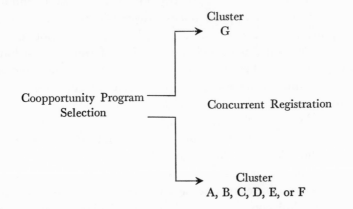

Following the frame of reference is a broadly stated program objective (macro defined outcome) which is designed to suggest to the student the type of opportunity available to him upon graduation from the program. A flow chart graphically portrays the options open to him during and after completion of the program. As suggested previously, at this stage not a word is mentioned about specific course requirements or program standards; rather, the whole focus is on helping the student decide upon a cluster that best satisfies his needs.

The Occupational, Commitment program is much the same as the traditional cooperative vocational education program currently practiced in many two-year colleges. It is designed for full-time students who have a clearly conceived career objective. The college provides a minimum of two years of course work in general and specialized education related to the student's work objective in conjunction with work experience supportive of his goal. A breadth of semiprofessional, technical, or middle-management two-year programs are offered in education, engineering, business, applied health, and community service areas. After the student has acquired the skills necessary to his employment, the college commits itself to provide placement for the student in a career area related to his interests. As in all coopportunity clusters, students are able to change clusters at will or to change career areas within a cluster.

At the completion of his program the student enters the labor force but has the option of returning for upgrading instruction at the community college or a nearby university (perhaps culminating in a bachelor of applied science degree in that career area). The opportunity of completing a bachelor's degree is not shut out to this student, since a smooth articulation of transfer (including work experience credits) is achieved between the cooperative education community college and the university. Occupational, Commitment is not a closed-ended program.

The second cluster, Occupational, Exploration, is very closely allied with cluster A but provides for greater flexibility. Students who select this cluster do so with the intention of shifting to cluster A before graduation. The program is designed especially for students who have an intense work orientation but are not at the time of admission able to declare a particular career objective and related preparatory program from coopportunity cluster A.

The program, at minimum a two-and-a-half-year program, explores career opportunities in broad areas that the student has singled out (allied health, business, engineering). Vocational guidance personnel meet with the student to review career options and assist the student in establishing career objectives. In addition to courses that present an occupational survey via field trips, guest lectures, and slide and tape presentations of career areas and related career programs, the college provides for varied work experiences through cooperative education. The objective of the program is to assist students in matching their personal drives and capabilities with careers that offer commensurate challenge and reward.

Coopportunity cluster C, Professional Orientation, is geared to those students who have clearly delineated career objectives in an area of professional responsibility. The student is told that many professional occupations require the completion of a bachelor's degree or special graduate degree programs and that the community college's mission in this regard is to supply a strong foundation of freshman and sophomore curriculum which introduces the profession and allows transfer to the university. Such careers as certified public accountant, social worker, lawyer, medical doctor, systems analyst, city planner, or market research investigator are typical of this category. The program stresses social science, humanities, and science curricula with some technical course work related to the student's area of professional interests. A key feature of this program is the alternation of study with work in agencies that offer experiences strategic to the professional functions that the student seeks ultimately to practice. A smooth articulation between the community college and the university is arranged for the student in this program. The need for semiprofessional and technical support personnel in this employment area is demonstrated to the student should he change his plans and decide to enroll in cluster A. The program is a minimum of two years in duration.

Program cluster D, Occupational, Advancement, is specifically designed for the full-time employee who desires retraining or advancement in an occupation. General education and specialized technical courses are offered in the afternoons and evenings and on Saturdays. Two degree programs are offered. One is a certificate-of-completion, a shortened, technically based program requiring a minimum of two years; the associate degree program, which is a minimum of three and a half years in duration. Both programs are heavily vocational and are structured around a cooperative education plan. College coordinators meet with the student's employer to help demonstrate the student's desire to advance in the organization, and to this end the college attempts to secure job rotation and occasional released time for the employee to enroll in classes. The student receives credit for his work experiences. Program offerings parallel the engineering, business, applied health, and community service areas offered in cluster A. In addition, the cluster D program can be geared to provide the emphasis of clusters B, C, E, F, or G should special student needs arise.

Coopportunity cluster E, Personal Development, Intellectual Exploration, is designed for students who are not currently interested in training for a particular career area but who want to explore various subject areas in the sciences, humanities, and social sciences. The student's educational objective is personal development and exploration, with perhaps the option of later study at a university in liberal arts or a professional curriculum. The college structures a pattern of work and study alternation, requiring a minimum of two years, and the program is arranged to be fully transferable. The core of general education courses may be supplemented with occupational survey courses at the student's discretion. The student's work experiences are purposely varied to provide a breadth of experiences. Should a work-experience period suggest an area of career interest, the student can easily change his program to cluster A, selecting a suitable technical, semiprofessional, or middle-management training area. Students in coopportunity cluster E meet frequently during the quarter with guidance and counseling personnel to narrow down a discipline of study or occupational interest for further pursuit at the community college or upon transfer to a university.

Coopportunity cluster F is also a "Personal Development" program, but with a "Goals Identification" orientation. Students entering this program have not decided upon an educational, personal, or career direction. An interdisciplinary two-year program, including a survey of occupational opportunities and regular sessions with the guidance and personnel staff to identify possible areas of study and occupational pursuit, is the focus of this program. As with cluster E, varied work experiences are provided the student. The objective of cluster F is to assist the student in the development of an educational plan and the selection of one of the previous clusters. A student would not actually complete his program of study in coopportunity cluster F.

Cluster G, Personal Development, Basic Skills, provides instruction in basic mathematics, English, or reading skills necessary for successful scholastic performance at the college. As in all clusters, cooperative education is integral to the program, and the work experience is related to the student's selected area of interest. For example, if the student is interested in a career in data processing, he concurrently registers in cluster A, the semiprofessional and technical program area. His first quarter of study, in the developmental or basic-skills areas, is followed by a cooperative period in a job related to or supportive of a data processing career. The student may spend from one to three quarters in cluster G before progressing to his designated program interest. Guidance and counseling services are provided on a continuing basis to this student, since he is especially prone to withdraw. The student is asked to meet with the advisor associated with his permanent cluster so as to foster a sense of progress and identification with his educational objectives.

Phase II: Operational Aspects

The relationship between the instructional staff and the centralized cooperative education department is that of staff authority. However, the centralized cooperative education staff department must have a close liaison with student service and instructional areas, a liaison facilitated by a carefully developed communications system. The effectiveness of faculty coordination in this model is contingent upon the services provided by the office of the dean of cooperative education.

Many faculty members in the hypothetical comprehensive cooperative education community college are designated instructor-coordinators, since their responsibilities are divided between coordination and classroom teaching. Students are assigned to faculty members at the rate of six students per quarter hour, or eighteen students per three quarter hours; and for these eighteen students the coordinator instructs a one-hour contact class (career practicum). A typical faculty member's load is nine hours of in-class instruction and three hours of work-experience credit (coordination of roughly eighteen students and the instruction of a career practicum). The college follows an alternating block plan. That is, each student is part of a team, wherein one student has a study period while the other student is working full time. Some selected faculty members devote full time to teaching, having a load of fifteen credit hours; others carry heavier coordination loads with a commensurate reduction in classroom instruction. Coordination overloads are occasionally granted at the rate of eighteen students per three quarter hours of credit. The central cooperative education staff department, upon communications from department or division chairmen, assigns students to instructor-coordinators and provides a list of employers who have indicated a willingness to participate in the program.

The director of the cooperative education department reports directly to the dean of student services and operates in close liaison with guidance, financial aid, registration, and placement offices. However, the primary responsibility of the dean and his department in the hypothetical model is in providing support functions to instructor-coordinators throughout the college. The cooperative education director has no line authority over faculty coordinators, who are directly responsible to their respective division and department chairmen.

The functions of the central staff are extremely varied. One important function is the collection of data about students and community. This data-collection process should begin with the administration of a student survey (see Chapter Four) designed to ascertain the needs and demographics of prospective students in the community college district. From this survey a needs profile is constructed and compared to the needs taxonomy reflected in co-opportunity clusters. In addition, a survey is made of the various organizations and institutions in the community, in order for the college to obtain a broad picture of employment opportunities. This survey is designed to ascertain employers' familiarity with the college's cooperative education program, the scope and character of their employment, and the nature of their training requirements.

The cooperative education administrator in the model community college is in a very important sense a public relations specialist. Specifically, the dean of cooperative education promotes the values of the program to the community at large, through meetings with professional and service organizations and informational letters and promotional pieces directed to employers. His efforts are critical in pioneering new employers. In addition, he represents the college in cooperative education meetings and conventions. His persuasive abilities must also come into play in organizing a cooperative education advisory committee. Recruiting solid, substantial community representatives to this advisory committee can add immeasurably to program success, and it is his responsibility to create and mold the conditions for the smooth and effective operation of this group in guiding the overall program. He and his staff also design and write the cooperative education student handbook, as well as a cooperative education newsletter.

The dean of the community college's cooperative education department is first and foremost a staff administrator (without line authority over faculty coordinators) who must provide or make ready the major ingredients of the cooperative education experience. Basically he and his staff have a two-pronged responsibility: on the one hand, they try to find new work positions and to upgrade existing positions through employer-development programs; on the other hand, they assign these work positions to appropriate instructor-coordinators. Also, in liaison with guidance personnel, they direct students to instructor-coordinators. The staff department is responsible for the regulation and allocation of the appropriate number of students and work positions based upon information from the division chairmen on instructor-coordinator loads.

Central cooperative education staff members also plan and assist in instruction of preemployment classes (career-orientation classes), which lay the groundwork for the employment or work experience during the succeeding quarter at the college. As an administrator, the director of cooperative education is responsible for the overall cooperative education program planning and control; his recommendations carry great weight with both deans of student services and academic affairs. As a part of his control responsibility, the cooperative education administrator assists in carrying out process and product evaluations. He administers student follow-up surveys to determine the progress that students are making toward their life goals (or changes in those goals) and their present educational and occupational status.

The instructor-coordinators carry out the program and work closely with the students in planning their personal, occupational, and educational goals. Each student completes a student information form, discusses his goals with his assigned instructor-coordinator, and examines possible work positions for the work period. This instructor-coordinator acts as the student's permanent educational advisor, meeting with him at least twice each quarter. At the outset the instructor helps the student plan a complete program of study for his tenure at the college, including the required career-orientation class and the required career practicum during the work period.

The coordinator, having a list of suggested work positions from the central cooperative education office, reviews these alternatives with the student the quarter prior to his work experience. When the student is sent out to inerview with the employer, he takes along a card of introduction which doubles as a return postcard to the college to notify the coordinator of the employer's acceptance or rejection of the student.

Shortly after the student begins work, the coordinator visits the work station and, in consultation with the employer and student, establishes defined outcomes for the work period. At this time any special questions or problems are discussed, and all three parties sign the training agreement clarifying their responsibilities to the program. The coordinator makes himself available for consultation throughout the quarter and establishes a particular date to return to pick up a defined-outcomes form from the student and the employer; the form, made out in triplicate, provides space for evaluation of the attainment of the learning objectives. The employer is asked to suggest ways in which the college can aid the student's development—perhaps through enrollment in particular classes at the college. At the end of the quarter the student files an end-of-work-period report reviewing the conditions of the job that quarter.

The instructor records comments made during his visits to the work station on a visit report form. He also completes a weekly report form and an expense account form and turns them in to the department or division chairman. The visit report is placed in the student's file along with any additional comments about his performance. At the end of the year the coordinator submits to his immediate supervisor an annual report, reviewing his activities for the year and summarizing the various visit reports. Each department and division chairman compiles these reports and, in turn, writes one final cooperative education report for the year in his program area.

The instructor-coordinator has certain other responsibilities which are essential to an efficient program. One such responsibility is instruction of the career practicum during the period of the student's work experience. The practicum is an informal seminar class in which the students discuss common problems and experiences; each student also is required to submit a written report in which he relates his personal goals and classroom instruction to his work experience. At the completion of the practicum the coordinator evaluates the practicum report and the achievement of learning objectives and decides on a grade for the student for the term. Periodically, throughout both work and study quarters, the student is invited to the coordinator's office to discuss progress toward the student's educational aims. An interview appointment card and an interview report are useful forms for facilitating this meeting. The latter form should also be placed in the student's file.

The instructor-coordinator meets with his own program or discipline advisory committee and occasionally sits in with the larger cooperative education advisory committee. While he does not have specific responsibility for pioneering work stations, he communicates freely with the central cooperative education office about potential work positions. Finally, an openness about cooperative education problems, issues, and possible innovations is achieved by regular meetings with other coordinators and the cooperative education director.

All reports and records alluded to in the previous paragraphs are presented in Exhibit A at the end of the book.

Potentials
and
Pitfalls

★★★★★★★★★★★★★★★★★★★★★★★★★★★★★★★★★★★★
★★★★★★★★★★★★★★★★★★★★★★★★★★★★★★★★★★★★

The continued growth of cooperative education at the community college is conditioned upon demonstrable values—values to the student, to the employer, to the college, and to the community. Outlined on the following pages are values that cooperative education has the potential for providing, along with a discussion of some of the main problems experienced in some programs.

Values to Student

Helps the student decide on a career. Cooperative education permits the student to "try out" a career area and to determine its applicability to his own interests and abilities. Even a work experience which is not wholly satisfactory to a student may be of important educational value, since he is better prepared to make a more enlightened career choice.

Increases potential placement, advancement, and remuneration. Students in cooperative education frequently remain with the employer they trained under, advance faster, and upon graduation are paid more than traditional students (Fager, 1969; Lindenmeyer, 1967; Smith, 1965; Marks and Wohlford, 1971).

Accentuates the importance of assuming responsibility. Cooperative education students must accept responsibility for their actions as a condition of employment in light of the authority that is delegated to them to perform company tasks. Employers hold cooperative students accountable for work performed in much the same way as full-time employees.

Sensitizes students to academic performance and staying in college. Students enrolled in cooperative education see new relevancy in their classroom instruction. Comparisons of grade point average and attrition rates reveal a superior performance for the cooperative education students over other students (Lindenmeyer, 1967; Smith, 1965; Gore, 1972; Marks and Wohlford, 1971). In addition, Baron (1968) studied fourteen demographic variables as they relate to academic performance of community college students and found that only two variables are strongly correlated to academic success; one of these variables is work experience.

Instills cognitive and attitudinal skills critical to successful job performance. Cooperative education students have the special advantage of interrelating classroom and work experiences in the development of logically conceived, well-grounded, personal work habits. Job performance becomes a reality and not some vague concept which may be understood only abstractly in the classroom.

Provides a matching of job to personal needs. Work positions are selected because of their relevance to students' needs and objectives. Accordingly, students' capabilities and interests are matched with work tasks to maximize educational impact.

Sensitizes students to interpersonal relationships. Cooperative education students via their work experience become aware of formal and informal organizational relationships and the importance of human relations. In particular, they learn how to get along with personnel integral to the organization as well as those serviced by it.

Supplements financial resources. Wages earned during the co-op period can serve as a means of financing the community college education and can give students, especially the economically disadvantaged, a sense of worth and economic independence which can be enormously self-fulfilling (Gore, 1972; Dawson, 1971).

Decreases the sense of isolation of the culturally and economically deprived student. The disadvantaged student in particular benefits from cooperative education, since he is able to acquire, with the efforts of the college, positions of responsibility that he probably could not otherwise obtain (Dawson, 1970). Involvement in the mainstream of community economic and social activity is particularly significant to this student's self-esteem and ability to contribute meaningfully to the total community.

Provides direct contact with practitioners. Students work with practitioners in the field and observe first hand what is necessary to success in that occupation. As a result of these contacts, they may receive referrals for permanent employment upon graduation. In addition, they will receive instruction from practitioners in techniques that cannot be learned in the classroom, thereby augmenting their theoretical learning.

Demonstrates the importance of formal education to work performance. According to a study by Leuba (1964), cooperative education contributes ideal conditions whereby students can relate classroom learning to many situations in the world outside the classroom. As a result, they appreciate—probably much more than other students do—the contributions of in-class instruction to performance in the work situation.

Fosters understanding of the subtleties of the managerial activity in problem solving. Cooperative education allows the student the opportunity to observe such important managerial dimensions as decision making, planning, organizing, and controlling under actual conditions as they relate to effective work performance.

Facilitates a study-work intermingling for lifelong learning. Cooperative education initiates a mixture or pattern of work and study which many educators feel is desirable, not just in the short run for an associate degree, but in the long run for lifelong learning.

Bridges the generation gap. The students' contact with a range of adults while on the job allows for the diminishing of differences between generations, since all personnel work together in the achievement of work objectives.

Allows for the development of critical social skills in a work setting. Cooperative education students observe first hand the importance of dress, grooming, punctuality, courtesy, poise, and clear and concise language to job success. These are skills that cannot be readily learned in the classroom of a college campus.

Aids the adjustment to work and the achievement of higher-level needs. Fitting in as an integral part of the larger society is a major concern of students, but cooperative education allows for a smoother articulation from college to work (Horn, 1971) and provides a better notion of work's relationship to the achievement of needs (Rowe, 1970).

Values to the College

Provides a college-community interchange. By virtue of a cooperative education program the college and the community interrelate on a scale never before realized. Not only are students interacting with the community's primary economic, political, and social institutions but faculty and staff are necessarily involved in the interchange of learning and practice (especially if faculty carry out the coordination function).

Improves student retention. A number of studies (Lindenmeyer, 1967; Smith, 1965; Gore, 1972) reveal that students enrolled in cooperative education programs are less inclined to drop out of college than traditional students are. The variety of classroom and out-of-classroom experiences, coupled with an involvement in the reality of the real world, strengthens the student's ties to his education.

Provides outside facilities that cannot easily be duplicated on campus. Cooperative education allows the college to draw upon the resources and facilities of the whole community at no expense to the taxpayer.

Achieves greater responsiveness to need. The close partnership between the college and the employer made possible by cooperative education results in a greater responsiveness of program and curricular offerings to the needs of the community.

Facilitates counseling. Under the cooperative plan, students are encouraged to establish realistic goals as a part of their placement on a cooperative job. The counseling process takes on a new vitality as students begin to actively formulate personal and career choices.

Clarifies the college function to the community. Members of the community, through their contacts with the college, become increasingly cognizant of the community college philosophy, purposes, programs, and services.

Familiarizes employers with the skills of community college students. Employers are able to observe first-hand the capability of community college students in performing work tasks, applying knowledge, and accepting authority.

Focuses on the student process of making career choices. Cooperative education, offered as a comprehensive program in both occupational and general education curricula, moves the college significantly ahead in guiding students to career objectives, enabling them to plan their studies more realistically.

Provides for an ongoing self-renewal of faculty. The college staff is constantly kept abreast of the latest developments and innovations in the community. College decisions concerning curriculum and instruction are conditioned on the most current and up-to-date information in the field. Moreover, contacts with practitioners make the faculty more knowledgeable. (For details about a specific program designed to develop a different kind of teacher for the community college, see Dawson, 1971.)

Makes for effective use of resources. College facilities are more economically used on a twelve-month basis with students alternating attendance at the college with work experiences off campus. Considerable economic advantages have occurred to some colleges making use of this plan, especially in a mandatory program (Knowles and Wooldridge, 1971, pp. 287–316; Rauh, 1971). Cost-effectiveness studies of the exemplary California program reveal that the program is "highly productive for the funds invested" (Bennett and Redding, 1972, p. 3).

Allows for immediate feedback regarding program success. The college—via feedback through cooperative education personnel, students, and employers—is better able to evaluate curriculum, teaching, advising, and other aspects of program success. The adequacy of programs can be judged on a regular and continuing basis.

For example, on the basis of feedback from its cooperative education staff, La Guardia Community College has significantly altered the direction and scope of its data processing program.

Recruits new students. Students and parents alike are attracted to community college cooperative education programs. Interestingly, La Guardia Community College has discovered that the predominantly blue-collar workers in this community—people traditionally negative toward college education but positive toward the work ethic—were persuaded to encourage their children to attend the community college because of the benefits of a work orientation afforded by cooperative education.

Benefits to the Community

Provides a pool of college-educated workers. Cooperative education students have demonstrated their understanding of the community's social and economic structures and are more readily adaptable to local needs. They are better prepared to assume positions of authority and intelligently contribute to the solution of community problems and to the economic well-being of the community.

Increases rapport between college and community. The college and community form a strengthened bond in a new partnership where each is more respectful and understanding of the other's mission. The notion on the part of some citizenry that the community college is a "fortress" (Cohen, 1969, pp. 61–67) in defense of and at odds with the "great unwashed" is dispelled under cooperative education.

Increases students' sense of citizenship and responsibility. Students who are participants in the community's economic and social institutions are more sympathetic with and sensitive to its authority relationships and decision processes. Therefore, in contrast to many traditional students, cooperative students hope to achieve positions of community responsibility in order to modify or contribute to the effectiveness of decision making in technical, social, political, or economic realms. The cooperative student finds it difficult to assume a passive role because he is a part of the community's day-to-day activity (Knowles, 1971, p. 51).

Increases the likelihood that students will remain in the community. Students enrolled in the cooperative program are assimilated into the community prior to graduation—not after graduation. The student develops a strong community orientation as he studies and practices in the community environment.

Introduces students to community opportunities. Through the partnership of college and community, students are provided the opportunity to sample from a spectrum of career opportunities. The community is offered the unique medium of the cooperative education program to present itself to promising students.

Provides preparatory training for middle-management, semiprofessional, and technical employment. The two-year college's occupational programs are geared to the provision of semiprofessional middle-management training, which is the fastest-growing sector of the labor force (Harris, 1964). The community benefits from the availability of a superior group of young persons to assume positions of responsibility in community institutions.

Values to the Employer

Provides students who have occupational experience and who may become permanent employees. The employer is provided with an employee who is college educated and predisposed to his company's functions and objectives. The student while completing his studies is familiarized with the subtleties and nuances of performing at an effective decision-making level.

Allows for careful screening of trainees. The employer can observe and measure students as trainees prior to full-time employment. He is able to ascertain the student's effectiveness and is better prepared to determine his employability on a full-time basis.

Provides a training program. Some large employers can more economically train new employees through the community college than they can through in-house instruction. In addition, small firms unable to provide a formal training program may, in partnership with the community college, supply their needs for qualified and experienced workers.

Reduces employee turnover. An employee who has progressed through a community college cooperative program has already examined the degree of fit of the job, and his decision to accept full-time employment is based on a compatibility of relationships and not mere chance. Therefore, he is less likely to leave his job than is an employee who has not had the advantage of cooperative education.

Provides a trainee with a curriculum geared to his employment area. Many cooperative students are enrolled in college studies which are directly related to their work. That is, their theoretical preparation is synchronized with their occupational exposure in preparation for a particular responsibility.

Allows the employer to influence the tenor of the college program. The employer, as a partner in the cooperative education endeavor, can offer advice and suggestions for important changes or needed innovations in curriculum through his contacts with instructor-coordinators.

Provides a highly motivated source of temporary or seasonal part-time employment. Students in a cooperative program are positively inclined toward the work responsibility because of its relationships to their educational objectives and career interests. Given this orientation, the student is responsive to in-class and on-the-job instruction and is anxious to carry out authority delegated to him.

Contributes in a positive way to community good will. The employer, by his participation in the community college cooperative program, assists in the development of the community's youth. He achieves good will for his actions and contributes in a socially responsible way to his community.

Provides a professional counseling staff for trainees. Under a cooperative program, the employer has the added advantage of drawing upon the college counseling staff in the solution of personnel problems involving college trainees.

Provides a means of recycling employees who are in need of additional educational training. The employer's full-time staff can be encouraged to attend the community college in a special cooperative arrangement. San Mateo Community College District offers an evening college cooperative program with local employers whereby full-time employees secure credit for their work experience while enrolled in evening college classes.

Releases highly trained employees from basic or elementary tasks. The employer can assign more highly trained and specialized personnel to complex skill tasks while utilizing the cooperative student in less complex areas better suited to the student's development.

Problems

Problems frequently identified with cooperative education operation tend to fall into one of four broad categories. The first involves the effect of economic and employment factors on the development of occupational opportunities. The second involves the impact of the placement on student life; the third, closely related to the second, involves the educational validity of the program. The fourth problem area concerns certain subtleties of cooperative education administrative practice.

Economic and employment variables. The first problem category has two parts: (1) the influence of the economic environment on occupational availability and (2) the impact of employment restrictions on placement. It would be naïve to assume that the quantity and quality of placements remain constant throughout the fluctuation of the business cycle. However, it is equally erroneous to assume that a serious business downturn means disaster for cooperative education. Amidst the sluggish economy of the early 1970s the number of placements and community colleges offering cooperative education programs increased. Most notably, La Guardia Community College in Queens, New York, initiated a mandatory program during the high-unemployment period of 1971–1972 and was able to place all students. The crucial influence is the existence of an aggressive and conscientious coordination effort with a close working relationship with employers. However, the coordinator is likely to be less effective when confronted with employment restrictions imposed by contracts or union regulations. (The material on forecasting and planning in Chapter Four and coordination activities in chapters Six and Seven addresses this class of problems.)'

Economic environment is a critical factor impinging on program success. Wilson and Lyons (1961, pp. 149–154) report that an employer's decision to take on student trainees is conditioned in part by the tenor of the economy. Approximately half of those employer surveyed suggested that the recession, which occurred prior to the study, influenced the number of students they were able to hire. (Also see Koos, 1970, p. 479.) Employment for community college students may also be limited by hiring restrictions imposed by the government or by unions (Billings, 1970, pp. 60–61; Wilson and Lyons, 1961, pp. 149–154; Barlow, 1963, pp. 56–57). Portman (1970) raises the ethical question of placing students in work positions during periods of high unemployment when disadvantaged persons desperately need work.

Student-placement variables. The planning of student placements is the second area of potential problems. What appears on the surface to be a relatively simple task of providing jobs for students is in fact a very complicated process involving the conscientious attempt to individualize particular experiences to specific student needs. These complicating factors include the appropriateness of the placement (the needs of students for particular jobs); its degree of challenge; its geographic proximity to student (as well as the coordinator); the elimination of certain student activities because of work obligations; the needs of employers for student trainees; the problem of scheduling classes convenient to students during study periods; and, most important, the need for balance between employer and student needs. Successful placement qualitatively should strive for a challenging and needs-satisfying experience for students *and* the satisfaction of employer need for capable workers (see Chapter Seven).

Placements provided for students may not always offer optimum conditions. Some students complain that they are offered only repetitive and menial jobs; and a number of studies (Bonnell, 1964, pp. 25–26; Wilson and Lyons, 1961, pp. 149–154; Hayes, 1969, pp. 16–19; Barlow, 1963, pp. 56–57) tend to support that complaint. Moreover, some cooperative education observers (Koos, 1970, p. 479; Portman, 1970) argue, participation in such a program reduces the student's ability to participate fully in college life and even reduces the time spent in classroom instruction. Certain logistics and scheduling problems also may occur because of outlying geographical placement of students (see D. Billings, 1970, pp. 60–61; E. R. Billings, 1971; Johnson, 1969, pp. 68–69).

Educational-validity variables. The challenge to educational validity manifests itself in many forms. Critics can argue that some placements are not related to the educational objectives of students, that some employers fail to rotate students and thus do not provide a breadth of experience, that some firms may encourage students to drop out of school, and that some students may come to regard practical experience as always superior to classroom studies. Critics might also argue that some students co-op primarily for financial remuneration, that some students may not see any relationship between their work and their studies, and that some colleges may not grant degree credit for the work experience. Still other critics will fault cooperative education because of the ineptness of its coordination. These problems are extremely serious, calling into question the very basis of cooperative education. (Techniques for guarding against these pitfalls are suggested in Chapters Seven and Eight.)

At the heart of these criticisms is the view that too often there is a weak relationship between study and work activities (see Koos, 1970, p. 479; Rauh, 1971, p. 13; Johnson, 1969, pp. 68–69; Barlow, 1963, pp. 56–57; Bonnell, 1964, pp. 25–26). Criticisms are also offered as to the variety of experiences students are able to have with a single employer. Barlow (1963, pp. 56–57), for instance, reveals the tendency of employers to limit a student to one narrow function instead of giving him exposure to a number of different jobs. Other problems are identified with the employer and his potential for limiting educational value. Barlow (1963) and Hayes (1969) point out that some employers may encourage students to work full time, causing them to drop out of school. Plachta (1969) observes that the employer can influence the student to place too much emphasis on "what is the current practice" rather than "what should be the current practice"; the student may be encouraged to feel the practitioner is always right and in fact superior to his "ivory tower" teacher.

The inability of the program to integrate study and work components may manifest itself in a student with a dual personality —a campus personality and a work personality, and these two personalities may never be seen as interrelating (Leuba, 1964, p. 5). Finally, the educational values of cooperative education may escape students who view the work experience as only a means of financial aid. This preoccupation with finances is cited in various studies and analyses (Johnson, 1969, pp. 68–69; Wilson and Lyons, 1961, pp. 149–154; Hayes, 1969, pp. 16–19; Bonnell, 1964, pp. 25–26).

Most if not all of the previously noted problems could be solved given adequate coordination, but the supervisory talents of coordinators vary widely. Johnson (1969) points to the dilemma of inept coordinators (and employers) whose supervisory skills are not up to the task. Bonnell (1964, pp. 25–26) warns that coordination which is not carefully performed may result in students who "merely mark time and end up with in inferior education." The coordination function is especially critical for a liberal arts student, whose work assignment is more difficult to match to his educational objectives.

Discussions of cooperative education and its associated educational values lead ultimately to the process for evaluating students (see Brown, 1971, pp. 25–27) and the resultant granting of credit toward graduation (see D. Billings, 1970, pp. 60–61; Wilson, 1973, pp. 28–38). Among evaluation procedures, employer feedback, coordinator input, and written reports are probably the most popular. Regarding the granting of credit toward degree requirements, the recognized educational value of cooperative education would seem to justify the granting of such credit. Unfortunately, however, some schools do not yet allow degree credit for this experience (see Chapter Eight).

Administrative variables. The fourth problem area is the result of certain administrative inefficiencies. Central to this administrative breakdown is a lack of commitment—primarily from ranking college officers but also from staff departments, faculty members, and the community. A second breakdown, and related to an important extent with the first, is communications—internally and, especially important, externally (promotion of the values of cooperative education). Critics also point to dissatisfactions that some employers register about its administration. Staffing is brought into question by others. Certainly the complexity of the cooperative education effort places special requirements for an effective administrative team, and in Chapters Four (planning and control), Five (organizing), and Seven (promotion) suggestions are offered for avoiding the kinds of administrative dilemmas suggested in the following paragraphs.

As indicated, this category of problem is related to a broad cross section of administrative breakdowns involving faculty, coordinators, employers, and students. In fact, as Barlow (1963) points out, it even involves problems in advisory committee operation. Administrative breakdowns in the area of cooperative education are sometimes the direct result of a lack of firm commitment by high-ranking college administrators (D. Billings, 1970, pp. 60–61) and sometimes the result of poor communication systems between coordinators, instructors, and employers (Barlow, 1963, pp. 56–57).

Faculty resistance to the intrusion of cooperative education is also an important administrative concern. In particular, Barlow suggests that vocational cooperative education programs sometimes lack status among faculty members. Wooldridge (1964) discusses the historical precedent for such negative attitudes emanating from the faculty. He points out that at one time educators saw a meaningful college education as an association with a "community of scholars in the intellectual atmosphere of the campus" removed from the competition of everyday life; some faculty members regarded cooperative education as too trade-school oriented and antithetical to the professional status they desired. Some critics would argue that to some extent the problem still lingers today, because faculties do not always fully support the program (D. Billings, 1970, pp. 60–61). According to Wilson and Lyons (1961, pp. 149–154), this resistance often results in a passive faculty that does not interrelate student experiences with classroom theory in class discussions. Barlow (1963) attributes problems of this sort to incomplete understanding of the nature, objectives, and importance of work experience on the part of faculty members. Resistance to cooperative education can be attributed not only to particular administrators and faculty members but also to certain critical staff functions of the college. Donn Billings notes in particular the lack of full endorsement provided cooperative education by some guidance departments (1970, pp. 60–61). Additional administrative problems may occur because of the lack of full community support (D. Billings, 1970).

Numerous employer dissatisfactions have been experienced with regard to cooperative education: dissatisfaction with the work of student trainees (Johnson, 1969, pp. 68–69); dissatisfaction with students who switched firms from work period to work period rather than remaining with the firm for the entire educational program; dissatisfaction because students do not remain full time after graduation; and dissatisfaction because cooperative programs among colleges in the area have different starting dates (Wilson and Lyons, 1961, pp. 149–154). If these problems result in a lack of cooperation from employers (D. Billings, 1970, pp. 60–61), a program can be seriously delibitated.

A number of these administrative problems identifiable with employers, administrators, faculty members, and students are related to communications breakdowns. A particularly unique promotion problem exists between college and employer (see Vickrey and Miller, 1973, pp. 9–18). Wooldridge (1964) notes that an absence of trust and understanding between education and industry, especially in early periods of higher education in this country, produced a climate incompatible with cooperative education, since "businessmen felt that educators were cloistered in their ivory towers" and educators saw businessmen as "entirely profit motivated." In addition to encouraging faculty members to support cooperative education, the problem of communicating benefits to students confronts administrators (Barlow, 1963, pp. 56–57). Adoption of a mandatory program in existing facilities makes it necessary to recruit additional students to efficiently use spaces left vacant by co-oping students (Rauh, 1971, p. 13)'.

Other administrative problems cited in the literature include the selection of a coordinator and assignment of loads. Both Rauh (1971, p. 13)and Donn Billings (1970, pp. 60–61) make reference to the shortage of qualified coordinators. Koos states, "Without unusual competence of coordinators, the programs languish or fail" (1970, p. 479)'. Brown (1971, pp. 25–27)' points out that the selection of a coordinator is an extremely difficult task because of the prerequisite of a social skill capable of providing meaningful interaction with employers, students, and professional educators. He also cites the difficulty of arriving at an ideal student-coordinator ratio; some programs are run at 80 to 1 while others are 200 to 1. Calendars and patterns of alternation greatly influence this ratio.

Community college cooperative education has the potential for providing new and important benefits for students, employer, college, and community. It is clear that the mere provision for such a program does not automatically secure desired ends. Problems with staffing, communications, student campus life, employer relations, and quality occupational opportunities must carefully be accounted and planned for. The foregoing specification of problems can be used as an alert system useful in preventing program breakdowns.

In the following chapters an administrative network will be prescribed for preventing the kind of problems identified in this chapter. Procedural guidelines will be offered in the realm of organization, planning, promotion, and other tactically important program areas.

Planning for Cooperative Education

★★★★★★★★★★★★★★★★★★★★★★★★★★★★★★★★★★★
★★★★★★★★★★★★★★★★★★★★★★★★★★★★★★★★★★★

The director or dean of the community college cooperative education program must maintain a delicate balance amidst a set of
intervening program influences generated by employers, students,
and community. Few administrators in the community college must
serve so many subpublics and countervailing powers. For example,
in an optional cooperative education program, students can effectively dictate program success by their decision to enroll for work
experience credit; employers, if coordination is lackluster or program
administration haphazard, can choose not to participate in the
program; college administrators must be assured that the program's
operation is efficient and effective; and faculty must be convinced
of the program's educational relevance. Therefore, the cooperative

51

education dean has to be an astute administrator and a capable human relations specialist.

Setting Objectives

A hierarchy of objectives can be of particular value to the chief cooperative education administrator. Table 2 shows such a hierarchy.

Table 2

MODEL SERVICE OBJECTIVES FOR A
COMMUNITY COLLEGE COMPREHENSIVE COOPERATIVE EDUCATION
PROGRAM

PRIMARY SERVICE OBJECTIVE

The student will accomplish defined outcomes critical to the achievement of educational objectives (career exploration, personal development, career preparation, other educationally valid ends) via a program of experiential learning.

SECONDARY SERVICE OBJECTIVE

The employer will be provided with a pool of college-educated youth and adults trained in occupational specialties or academic disciplines and motivated to the performance of appropriate work standards supportive of the student's educational needs.

COLLATERAL SERVICE OBJECTIVE

A. The community will be provided with a college-educated citizenry familiar with and predisposed to the solution of pressing social, economic, and technological problems critical to community development.

B. The college will interact and share resources with the community.

C. The financing and economic integrity of the college will be fostered by efficient and effective administration of the cooperative education program.

Responsibility to the employer, while certainly not the primary objective, is so important as to be ranked immediately behind service to the student. Collateral service objectives rank with, but slightly below, the secondary service objective. These objectives include service to the community's social, economic, and cumulative manpower needs and the provision of efficient and effective operations so as to satisfy the economic needs of the college.

Establishing Premises for Planning

The planning of cooperative education, in both initial and ongoing phases, ought to be established on a network of premises about the community, its economic needs, specific manpower requirements, student orientation, student needs, and employer and student willingness to participate in the community college cooperative education program. Carefully administered surveys can be especially useful in establishing premises for the planning function. Community college educators responsible for comprehensive cooperative education programs can learn much from the initiative that vocational cooperative education has taken in fostering the use of surveys.

At one time the community survey, which provided data about employment needs and availability of work opportunities for students, was considered the essential research effort; the student survey was viewed as a necessary but secondary endeavor. However, a new conception of the importance and priority of community versus student survey is taking place (see particularly Wallace, 1970, p. 11). This is not to suggest that the community survey is any less valuable in designing and upgrading programs but rather that it is not the first step in the investigative process. The first step ought to be the gathering of information about the student clientele. The thrust of this reorientation is that students ought not be fitted to employer requirements but that work experiences should be selected and developed in support of student needs. The purpose of the community survey thus changes from "What part-time jobs can you offer to cooperative students?" to "What is the scope and dimension of your employment?" So that the college and employer can plan experiences supportive of particular student needs, the college should carefully analyze data from the community survey. The feedback provided from community surveys should be seen not only as a useful planning aid but as an important source of input to the vocational guidance activity.

With this reordering of survey procedure in mind, consider the kinds of information useful to cooperative education planning and some observations on appropriate surveys to collect the data. The student survey is designed to identify key demographic characteristics of potential students in the surrounding community. Several important clienteles need to be recognized and should accordingly be surveyed in the study; these clienteles include students from local high schools who are likely candidates for full-time admission, adults employed in local community institutions who would like to enroll in the evening college cooperative program, unemployed youths and adults who seek the development of a marketable skill, housewives who wish to expand their personal or occupational vistas, and returning veterans who might aspire to either full-time or part-time study at the community college. The survey should ascertain the following facts about the student: educational predisposition in terms of his personal development, career preparation, upgrading, retraining, or exploratory needs; interest in and understanding of a comprehensive cooperative community college program; work-experience needs; plans for study in higher education; area of occupational interests and aspirations; personal objectives; avocational goals; important personality characteristics; socioeconomic characteristics.

The community survey would sample institutions in industrial, governmental, educational, medical, commercial, and social realms. Its objective is to establish the firm's function and employment characteristics. The following types of information should be secured: name and title of person completing the questionnaire; type and nature of the enterprise; number of employees presently employed (critical shortages and why, anticipated increases or decreases, part-time versus full-time employment, employment of college youth); seasonal employment changes of the firm; entry-level jobs that might be opened to a community college student; likelihood of major changes in the firm's technology, purposes, or employment pattern; training programs currently provided by the company; the company's familiarity with the values of the cooperative education program; the company's desire to participate in the cooperative education program by hiring student trainees; the company's willingness to discuss with the college a means of partnership by which the college can contribute to the firm's needs for trained personnel and the firm can contribute to the education of the community's youth.

Data from this survey, taken cumulatively, provide an employment profile for the community and are useful in establishing planning guidelines. In addition, other sources of secondary data are available to the cooperative education administrator from the local Chamber of Commerce or the Superintendent of Documents, U.S. Government Printing Office in Washington. The following documents, for instance, are published by the Bureau of Labor Statistics: *Occupational Outlook Handbook* (published biennially; provides a complete presentation of the employment requirements and remunerations for most of the nation's occupational categories), *Occupational Outlook Quarterly,* Occupational Outlook Reprint Series (presents particular occupations and is excerpted from the handbook), *Dictionary of Occupational Titles* (provides an outline of the responsibilities of major occupational classifications), and *Manpower Report of the President* (published annually; suggests employment trends).

Both student and community surveys should be accompanied by a letter on a college letterhead explaining the purpose and objectives of the study. A mail questionnaire is normally called for, given the probable large sample size for community colleges in most metropolitan areas. A stamped, return envelope will increase the return measurably, and the questionnaire itself should be designed to be concise, clear, and easily completed. It should be field-tested and changed as necessary before the actual mailing. Follow-up letters should be prepared for those who did not respond to the survey.

Information gathered from both community and student surveys will add significantly to the quality of the cooperative education plan. This plan should be the culmination of a statement of premises based upon a whole series of inputs from faculty members, administrators, and students, from community surveys, advisory committees, state and federal government funding officials, and from all those related to or influenced by the cooperative education program. The plan should begin with a statement of philosophy (see Chapter One) and educational intent (see Chapter

Eight). From this point, all important program subsystems should be detailed, defined, and developed so as to suggest directions for the activities of cooperative education coordinators (see Exhibit A).

Financial Planning

The budget or financial aspects of cooperative education operation has special implications for community college administrators. Several subtleties of cooperative education budgeting are suggested by the following conditions: (1) An alternating block (alternating terms of study and work), mandatory program requires that the budget be prepared for a full calendar year of operation. (2) In order to fully utilize the physical plant, the college adopting a cooperative plan must substantially increase its freshman class in order to fill spaces left by late first-year students and second-year students who are alternating work and study periods. (3) The college can reduce overhead cost per student by spreading the total cost of cooperative education over a larger number of students, including those off campus during work periods. (4) Optional cooperative programs may increase total costs; additional courses (sometimes called trailer courses) may need to be offered in order to allow cooperative students to finish their degree (Knowles, 1971, pp. 221–224).

The former vice president of Antioch College, Morton Rauh (1971), conducted a financial analysis of two four-year colleges; one of these colleges offered a mandatory cooperative education program, and the other did not. His analysis was based on a yearly tuition for two work and two study quarters (which is the same as a three-quarter program in a traditional college), a 30 percent increase in teaching faculty, the addition of administrative and student service personnel, and a full-time cooperative education staff. Rauh found that the expenses of the cooperative college increased substantially (by one third) to accommodate an expanded student enrollment, but its revenue also increased—by two thirds over the other institution.

It is clear that economic advantages are greater if the program is mandatory rather than optional. In fact, an optional program may generate additional costs (for coordination, administration, support staff, promotion, and other program elements) sufficient to nullify increases in revenue. Student fees for cooperative education are the critical variable; if there are substantial enrollments, revenues should exceed expenses. The half-day alternation pattern used in many community college programs is not as financially sound a plan as the alternating block arrangement—unless it can be scheduled so that half of the cooperative students are programmed for work in the morning and studies in the afternoon and the other half have morning classes and afternoon work. In a mandatory program this allows the potential for a doubling of student enrollment and a greatly enhanced use of physical plant per student enrolled, as is achieved in a mandatory alternating block program. Financial rewards will accrue to those institutions which carefully plan for maximum use of coordinators, faculty, and support staff on a year-round educational program (Knowles and Wooldridge, 1971, pp. 288–289). A checklist for use in planning a financial budget is presented in Exhibit C.

Evaluative Procedures

Achieving cooperative education program objectives is dependent on the soundness of planning premises, the logic by which the plan is designed, and the integrity of the staff in its commitment to plan directives (assuming resource adequacy). Controlling for program variations and incompletely achieved objectives should be a major function of the cooperative education administrator activity. An evaluative procedure is necessary to determine if the program is on target in meeting its objectives. The large number of program variables (subsystems) complicates the task; nonetheless, it does not diminish its importance in assuring program payoffs for students and community.

The institutional research activity of the community college can aid in the retrieval and analysis of data about the cooperative program. To the extent that coordination is decentralized, the evaluation activity is logically the responsibility of the respective program and departmental areas with the assistance of the cooperative education staff department. Instructor-coordinators from each of the college's instructional areas would be active participants

in such an evaluation procedure. In California the passage of the
Teacher Evaluation Act has special implications for decentralized
cooperative education programs. Inputs from students, other faculty
members, administrators, and the instructor being evaluated are
sought in those institutions. Cohen and Brawer (1972, pp. 33a–
33d) have suggested four areas for faculty evaluation which also
have application to instructor-coordinators: instruction, including
the achievement of in-class objectives and work-experience objectives of student-learners; service to the college, such as participation
in college committees and service in various institutional activities;
service to the community; professional expertise, including all
activities initiated by the instructor-coordinator to improve his
knowledge of his work.

   Butler and York (1971)', addressing themselves to overall
program evaluation, call for a continuous and systematic evaluation
system. They suggest that the program should be evaluated in two
ways: measurement of student outcomes ("product" evaluation)
and evaluation of the effectiveness of the total program ("process"
evaluation)'. Process factors requiring evaluation include the following: achievement of broad program goals; adequacy of work
experiences; effectiveness of classroom instruction (practicum, orientation); suitability of administrative leadership; ability of instructor-
coordinators; adequacy of cooperative education forms and
paperwork; efficiency of organizational relationships; effectiveness
of guidance and placement; adequacy of budget; and availability
and value of supplies and support materials. A cost-benefit analysis
of the cooperative education program is useful to a process evaluation (D. Billings, 1970, p. 121). The costing out of a cooperative
education program is crucial (Knowles and Wooldridge, 1971,
pp. 287, 316), but complications arise from the difficulty of ascer-
taining the precise benefits of the program. This barrier is not in-
surmountable, and cooperative education administrators should be
encouraged to complete such an endeavor. In their second annual
report, representatives of the consortium of five California colleges
report on such a cost-effectiveness study (Bennett and Redding,
1972, p. 3)'.

   For successful completion of a process evaluation, the institution's philosophy, objectives, and cooperative program goals

should be the standard for measurement of the program. In addition, as wide a spectrum of persons associated with the program as possible should participate in the evaluation; desirably, advisory committee members, administrators, students, faculty members, and employers should be involved in the process. Internal data on file concerning students, employers, and the community may be useful to the evaluation endeavor. Especially important is an evaluation of the effectiveness of work positions and their respective employer-supervisors in providing educational values. Instances of ineffective program operation should be brought to the attention of the participating employer in order to ensure a high-quality program. Mason and Haines (1972, p. 257) suggest, "Every training station should be reviewed at the end of the school year. . . . The coordinator should return to the manager or job supervisor and say, 'Here is a picture of the opportunities for learning which were provided your student-learner last year. This was a fine effort. If similar experiences can be provided during the coming year, we would like to cooperate with you by sending you appropriate potential trainees for interview.' Or in some instances, the teacher-coordinator may have to return and say, 'Here is a picture of the limited learning experiences which were provided your student-learner last year. This narrow profile needs to be adjusted to a more representative training situation, and I hope you will help us use this situation as an educational experience for a student next year.' " Perhaps most important, the process evaluation of training positions, the coordination function, or any of a number of process elements should result in a revised and changed plan in order to better move to the attainment of program and college objectives.

Jerome Moss has emphasized the importance of evaluative criteria: "One of the most critical aspects of program evaluation, and the one which has thus far probably received the least attention, is the identification and measurement of the program outcomes which are to serve as evaluative criteria. Everyone affected by evaluation, and that is all educators, must be concerned with developing as complete an array of relevant potential outcomes as possible for use by evaluators" (in Wallace, 1970, p. 88). The following program outcomes are presented in question format by one cooperative education authority (D. Billings, 1970, pp. 126–127):

(*1*) *How many students who have received coop-erative instruction are employed in occupations for which they were trained, or are in related occupations? How long do they remain in their jobs?*

(*2*) *What are the unemployment rates of students who were in cooperative programs compared with the total population?*

(*3*) *Are the workers who received cooperative in-struction satisfactory to their employers and satisfied with their employment, and how does the adjustment of these workers compare with those who had a different educational background?*

(*4*) *What is the school retention rate of cooperative students as compared to the rate for students as a whole?*

(*5*) *How many students who wanted cooperative training and could benefit from it were served? Who were not served and how many were there?*

Moreover, the cooperative education administrator should not lose sight of student outcomes. We have here advocated that community college educators should provide a clear indication of the probable outcomes of their programs of study (based upon the premise that the student's decision to expend time, effort, and money for a community college education ought to be founded on a rather definite notion of the outcome of that experience). Simi-larly, it has been advocated that community college cooperative educators use the defined-outcomes approach during cooperative education work periods and related classes. To the extent that the college commits itself to a definition of outcomes for its students, it has made a major contribution toward carrying out a product or student evaluation. The measurement of actual performance with performance standards affords the cooperative educator a better notion of the program's success in meeting students' educational needs.

In addition, it is critically important that follow-up surveys of students and community be carried out. Students transferring to a university or planning immediate employment after graduation should be followed up by personal interview or survey to determine their current status. Longer-run studies to ascertain changes in employment, career advancement, educational achievement, and/or community activities should also be conducted.

The cost accountant's measuring stick—for comparing *standards* with *actual* performance in the determination of *variances* —has application in this evaluative procedure, especially to the extent that the college has committed itself to a specification of broad program outcomes (see the defined outcomes for coopportunity clusters in Chapter Two, Figures 1–7) ; these outcomes act as cooperative education standards. Follow-up survey data can be manipulated so as to establish a student profile (actual performance). Variances are ascertained by comparison of standards and actual.

The flow charting of options for each coopportunity cluster presented in the model program provides a useful basis for the comparison. What percentage of the graduates followed a career, life, or educational pathway suggested in the flow chart? Of this group, which pathway proved to be the most accessible, and which the least accessible? What percentage of graduates moved in pathways not suggested by the flow chart? Why? Which coopportunity cluster demonstrated the greatest achievement of prescribed outcomes? Which demonstrated limited or minimal achievement of defined outcomes? Why?

An Evaluation and Planning Model

The model shown in Figure 8 presents those variables which impinge upon the operation of an effective cooperative education program and which therefore require close attention in both planning and evaluative phases. As the model makes clear, community college cooperative education does not operate in a vacuum; instead, numerous environmental variables influence program operation and accomplishments. The environments suggested in the model include social environment, political environment, educational environment, technological environment, and economic environment. Even though the cooperative administrator has very

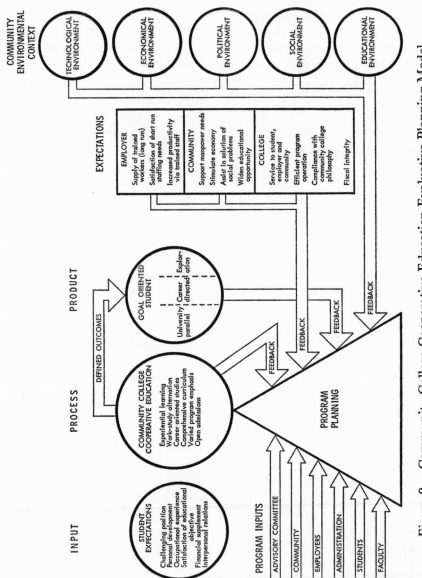

Figure 8. Community College Cooperative Education Evaluative Planning Model.

limited influence over any of these environments, it is important for him to secure a regular flow of information about each of them, so that he can better plan for a viable cooperative program.

Social environment refers to the traditions and values of the community in which the community college cooperative program is offered. More conservative communities, embittered by campus unrest nationally, may resent the encroachment of the college into the community; for example, the long-haired data processing major may enrage a prospective employer. Such stereotypes of "college" and "student" may require thoughtful communications to community power structures in order to pave the way for acceptance of the "college in the community" concept. Some cooperative education administrators have filled coordination positions to satisfy a preconceived notion of a white-shirted, straight-laced employer style, when in reality the rapid advancement of younger executives into key management posts has resulted in a considerably more flamboyant and colorful executive posture in some firms. In short, cooperative education administrators must keep the pulse of social and cultural community leanings. Participation by coordinators in the community's philanthropic, social, and professional organizations can heighten their sensitivity to social and cultural community patterns.

Economic environment is particularly important to the cooperative education coordinator. An otherwise strong cooperative education program may falter if a community experiences depressed conditions or a rapid business decline. Capital investments by businessmen and government spending in the public sector have a major impact on the community's economic livelihood. Cooperative educators must be sensitive to changes in the economy. Certain key industries are usually relied upon for numerous work positions. Therefore, a special effort should be made to observe key indices for those industries. The coordination practice of "putting all the eggs in one basket" can have a severe impact on a program in depressed times; feedback is all the more important under conditions of this type. Local chambers of commerce provide much data on these economic changes, and state employment bureaus provide employment spectrums useful to the coordination process.

The technological environment also deserves careful observation. Implementation of new equipment may suggest the need for new career courses or programs; the retirement of old machinery or processes may cause employment dislocation, requiring the college to pull back in some program areas or perhaps offer upgrading instruction for those workers who were displaced. Cooperative education feedback concerning changing technology is extremely useful for the planning activity carried out by occupational educators. Frequent visits to employers and participation in professional organizations is helpful in this respect.

Educational environment is simply the existence of other educational institutions offering a cooperative program in the community. Advances in vocational education funding provide for an increasing number of high schools offering cooperative programs. Other postsecondary institutions or adult classes given at the high school or by community social agencies may provide another source of competition. Nearby universities may offer cooperative education programs, and the cooperative education administrator needs to be alerted to all these possible sources of cooperative education competition. The coordinator should meet periodically with cooperative education representatives of these other institutions to share common problems and cooperate in the identifying and using employment opportunities.

The political environment of the community is important for the cooperative education administrator for two reasons: decisions by local, state, and national leaders may serve to create or eliminate training positions in local government agencies; and new laws, (social security, minimum wage, equal opportunity employment) can influence the conditions of the student's employment. The cooperative education administrator also needs to be sensitive to political moods created by politicians, because these can serve to alienate or reinforce rapport between the college and other environments, specifically the social and economic environments.

It is not suggested nor is it feasible that the cooperative education administrator hire political scientists, sociologists, or economists in order to stay attuned to these environments, but it is reasonable to assume that effective cooperative administrators can and should base their cooperative education plans on readily available information about community environments. Certainly the cooperative administrator can draw upon the knowledge possessed by the teaching faculty in each of these areas, especially if one of the environments looms large over program operation. In short, effective planning and evaluation should be product oriented; but process, expectations of those affected by the program, and environmental influences should be carefully accounted for.

Organization-in Cooperative Education

★★★★★★★★★★★★★★★★★★★★★★★★★★★★★★★★★★★★
★★★★★★★★★★★★★★★★★★★★★★★★★★★★★★★★★★★★

Organizing for cooperative education in the community college can take on varied forms. A distinction can be made between those programs which are centralized and those which are decentralized, between a pure coordination-function responsibility and a combined-function responsibility (responsibility for coordination and instruction); a distinction can also be made between autonomous cooperative education departments and those attached to one of the traditional community college functional areas. Community college organizations are traditionally structured around three major components: academic affairs, student services, and business management.

The academic affairs component is traditionally divided into university parallel and general education divisions, and an occupational division which is further segmented into various business, health, and engineering departments; community service and continuing education divisions are other organizational functions that might be placed under academic affairs. Student services typically include a whole range of activities, from guidance and counseling, testing, financial aid, and placement to student activities, including athletics. The business management organizational activity provides for the finance, accounting, and control functions typical of most educational institutions.

Organizational Alternatives

The decision as to where cooperative education ought to be placed in the organization is dependent on the mission and philosophy that the college conceives for itself and for the work experience program, as well as on the "personalities" within the administrative hierarchy. The following alternative organizational locations offer special advantages and disadvantages for community college administrators:

(1) Centralized administration and coordination as an adjunct to student services.

(2) Centralized administration and coordination as an adjunct to academic affairs.

(3) Centralized administration and coordination as an autonomous organizational activity having coequal authority with student services and academic affairs.

(4) Centralized administration in academic affairs and decentralized coordination as an adjunct to departmental and divisional instructional levels.

(5) Centralized administration in academic affairs and decentralized combined-function coordination at the departmental and divisional instructional levels. Coordination and instructional responsibilities are combined, in persons usually given the title of instructor-coordinator.

(6) Decentralized administration in an instructional branch of the college coupled with decentralized combined-function or separate-function coordination.

(7) Centralized administration in student services with decentralized coordination as an adjunct to departmental and divisional instructional levels, which may be either combined-function or separate-function.

Alternative (1), the centralization of the department in the student services area, allows for a close working relationship with placement, counseling, and financial aid personnel, but it limits a close identification with academic affairs in achieving a careful blending of work and study ingredients.

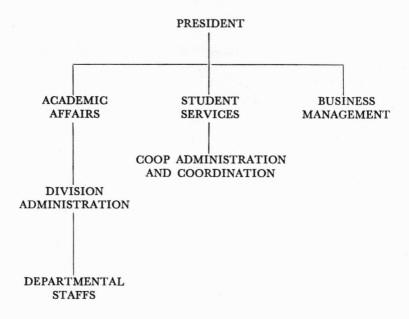

ORGANIZATIONAL ALTERNATIVE (1). Centralized administration and coordination as an adjunct to student services.

Alternative (2) provides for a closer rapport with the traditional academic endeavors, but because the coordination activity is centralized it is still removed from the instructional areas, and a close affiliation with counseling and other student services activities is sacrificed.

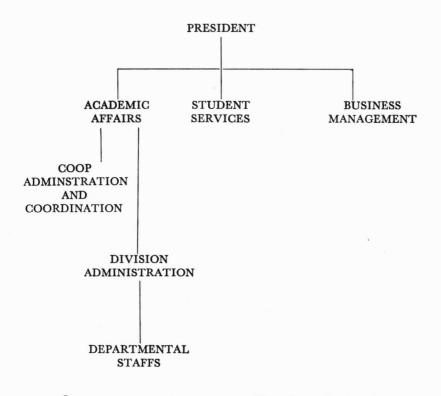

ORGANIZATIONAL ALTERNATIVE (2). Centralized administration and coordination as an adjunct to academic affairs.

Alternative (3) is characterized by the same weaknesses attributed to (1) and (2), but it has the special advantage of autonomy. This organizational placement reflects its relative importance to institutional goals and philosophy coupled with what is likely to be a strong administrative commitment to its purpose.

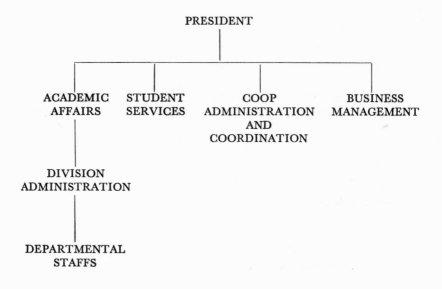

ORGANIZATIONAL ALTERNATIVE (3). Centralized administration and coordination as an autonomous organizational activity with coequal authority with student services and academic affairs.

Alternative (4) offers the special advantage of close rapport between traditional faculty members and cooperative coordinators, which makes possible a stronger bonding of work and study; its disadvantages include separation from the centralized department and having responsibility under two lines of authority, one leading to the instructional department and one to the cooperative administrator.

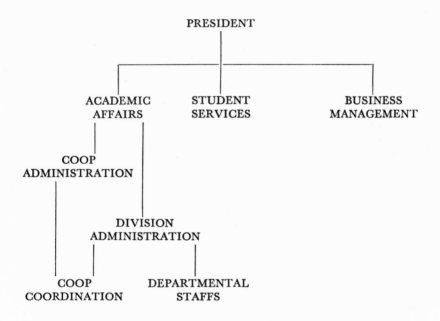

ORGANIZATIONAL ALTERNATIVE (4). Centralized administration in academic affairs and decentralized coordination as an adjunct to departmental and divisional instructional levels.

Alternative (5) has the same advantages and disadvantages as number (4), and it offers the special feature of combining instruction and coordination in the same person, which provides an extremely strong work and study integration for students as well as keeping the instructor alert to changes in his occupational specialty.

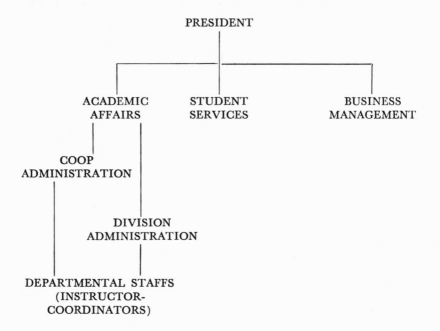

ORGANIZATIONAL ALTERNATIVE (5). Centralized administration in academic affairs and decentralized combined-function coordination at the departmental and divisional instructional levels.

Alternative (6) has advantages and disadvantages similar to (4) and (5), but by decentralizing administration it makes for a closer working relationship between coordinators and co-op program directors despite the disadvantages of fragmenting co-op (in effect creating many co-op education departments that are attached to program or discipline areas); Co-op typically thrives on a cross-fertilization of placements, avoiding the kind of competition between departments that is created here.

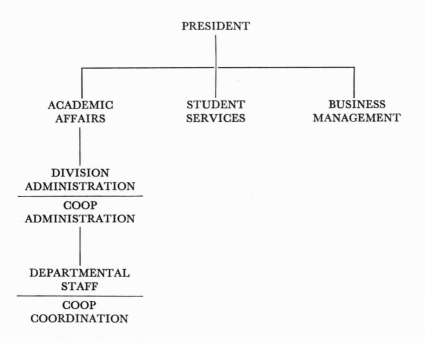

ORGANIZATIONAL ALTERNATIVE (6). Decentralized administration in an instructional branch of the college coupled with decentralized combined-function or separate-function coordination.

Alternative (7) maintains the advantage of a close rapport with student services and establishes the critical coordination function as a faculty responsibility; this insures a careful merging of work and study, but does so at the expense of additional administrative difficulties caused by dual lines of authority and separation of administrative and coordination functions.

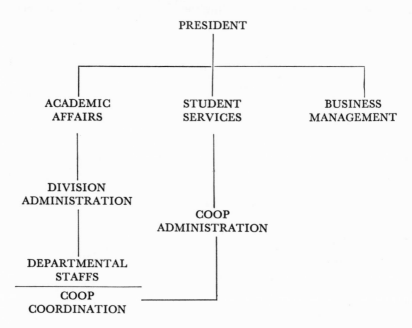

ORGANIZATIONAL ALTERNATIVE (7). Centralized administration in student services with decentralized coordination as an adjunct to departmental and divisional instructional levels which may be either combined or separate function.

Bostwick notes: "Cooperative functions either become centralized to provide more uniform control and efficient utilization of one or more coordinator's talents or disjointly operated dependently of the interest and available time of specific teaching faculty" (1972, p. 49)'.

Wilson's *Survey of Cooperative Education, 1972* (p. 12) reveals that 42.3 percent of two-year collegiate programs are organized as centralized departments reporting to an academic dean or vice-president; 39.4 percent are centralized programs with coordinators frequently attached to an academic department; roughly 6 percent report directly to the president; and 12.7 percent are under the auspices of student services. Wilson's statistics do not indicate the degree to which coordination is combined-function or separate-function, nor does it suggest the extent to which coordination is decentralized to an instructional level while cooperative education administration is centralized. These new patterns of cooperative education organization not only complicate the problem of gathering data on program operation but also confound community college administrators who are trying to decide on a cooperative education organization scheme.

Some would argue that a separate cooperative education function (alternative 3) with its own dean reporting directly to the president is "the best of all possible worlds." The differentiation of cooperative education as a distinct institutional function, the resultant achievement of autonomy, and provision for coequal authority with the major community college organizational functions would be primary advantages of such a plan.

La Guardia Community College in New York, which provides cooperative education for all of its students, operates under such an organizational arrangement. There is little question that this organizational placement clearly demonstrates cooperative education's institutional importance, but some possible disadvantages should be carefully considered. Assuming the importance of a close rapport between the cooperative education department and student services, counseling, and placement activities, in addition to the instructional arm of the college, a question must be posed: Can a separation from these areas foster closer liaison, or does it result in a greater demarcation of functional responsibilities? A small community college with a limited administrative hierarchy can operate very productively under such an arrangement because of the necessary interrelationship of administrative activities dictated by staff size and the reality of a physical plant that brings personnel into close contact. Community colleges experiencing rapid growth and expanding campus construction might find this organizational scheme less adaptable to their operational practices. In such a situation not only is authority divided but whole staffs are departmentalized and physically separated by the realities of space. This kind of growth could foster duplication of functions and diminished returns as cooperative education occupies its own bureaucratic niche apart from the placement service, the instructional staff, and guidance and counseling personnel.

Dudley Dawson, who has served as a consultant to community colleges, offers a differing perspective:

Locating the cooperative education department in the administrative structure depends greatly on local circumstances. In some situations it works best under the Dean of Instruction; in others, under the Dean of Student Services. Regardless of its organizational placement, the cooperative education department should have an easy and effective relationship with the faculty and staff under both Deans. In a large-sized college with many or all of its students in cooperative education it is preferable to have a Dean of Cooperative Education who on a coordinate level can secure effective liaison with the other Deans. . . . Because in the operation of cooperative education there needs to be day by day coordination with student counseling, student financial aid, admissions, registration, and other part-time and graduate placement [functions] (all of which are under the Dean of Student Services in most community colleges), it is often better to locate the Cooperative Education Department with the Dean of Student Services but with an established policy and functional relationship with the Dean of Instruction and his Academic Departments or Divisions. Regardless of the plan it is desirable to unite cooperative education administration with part-time student and graduate placement; otherwise, there is confusing and wasteful overlapping. Such unification will greatly strengthen the placement of all students and will improve the personnel services and the reception with employers. Finally, the location of the cooperative education function should be with a Dean who has interest and influence in its development throughout the college. (Personal communique)

The popular tactic of centralizing cooperative education under the dean of academic affairs is not altogether failsafe either, as suggested in the brief introduction to organizational alternatives. Coordination with student services becomes an important problem, and in reality the special value of affording a close relationship between cooperative and instructional staffs may be difficult to achieve because of a centralization of the coordination activity, especially in larger community colleges. Placement of cooperative education under student services offers difficulties of its own, because the coordination of work with study that is fostered by a strong relationship with faculty members is more difficult to attain. It is clear there is no single best organizational placement for cooperative education in the community college, but interesting modifications of existing organizational frameworks may provide some possible options for experimentation.

One rather unusual alteration of existing practice, as suggested in the introduction, is the centralization of cooperative education administration and the decentralization of coordination to the instructional level. Under such a plan, cooperative coordinators associate directly with and are considered counterparts to traditional faculty members, or in some instances faculty members have a combined teaching and coordinating responsibility. Totally cooperative vocational education programs in community colleges have typically operated under a plan of decentralization of cooperative education with an instructor-coordinator mode of staffing. The advantages of having an instructor coordinate the same students he instructs on a day-to-day basis are significant; such an arrangement provides for a more up-to-date and real-world orientation for faculty members and provides a closer integration of study and work experiences for students.

The five-college consortium of California community colleges experimenting with cooperative education uses a centralized administrative department reporting to the academic dean and a decentralized coordination staff. Cooperative coordinators are provided for under three patterns of staffing, which vary from college to college in the consortium. The first pattern is a voluntary part-time arrangement in which faculty members handle cooperative students as part of an overload system; the second is a release-time plan in which faculty members coordinate students along with handling their regular instructional responsibilities; and the third is full-time coordination responsibility. In the five colleges, coordination is not just a responsibility of occupational faculty members, for faculty members in history, English, sociology, psychology, and other fields are engaged in the coordination process in a truly comprehensive cooperative education program. This plan of decentralized coordination and centralized administration can be made to operate quite effectively, as the California plan demonstrates, but once again community college administrators have bought the advantage of a thoroughgoing merger of the cooperative education activity with the traditional classroom instructional activity at the price of a separation from student services and the administrative peculiarity of a dual line of authority (instructor-coordinators are in reality responsible for coordination to the co-op department and for instruction to their own division chairmen).

A college which places special value on the interaction of cooperative personnel with guidance, financial aid, and placement staffs but wishes to secure the advantages of decentralized coordination might wish to consider the applicability of a centralized cooperative education office in the student services area but with the coordination function performed by personnel (preferably, faculty members) attached to the instructional branches of the college. (This is the organizational strategy suggested in the model in Chapter Two.) This kind of arrangement would effectively bridge the gap between student services and academic affairs, but it would be complicated by the possibility of a strained administrative chain of command whereby administration and coordination functions are separated.

All of the organizational alternatives set forth here have certain limitations, and this plan is no different, but intelligent administration can guard against a strained authority relationship by carefully distinguishing between line and staff responsibilities. While there are certain administrative risks, the potential rewards are significant: close relationships are nurtured between both major functions of the college (academic affairs and student services); faculty members become active participants in the cooperative education activity; instructional deans have primary responsibility for *all* aspects of the student's education (not just classroom studies); and placement, counseling, and other student service activities are coordinated with cooperative education.

Under such a plan, faculty members have responsibility for the in-class and out-of-class dimensions of the student's education. The dichotomy between cooperative education coordinators and teaching faculty members is diminished, because faculty members participate in the placement of students in suitable work positions (as determined by their personal, intellectual, exploratory, or career objectives). The establishment of learning objectives and their evaluation extends from the classroom to the work site.

This approach would delegate to the central cooperative education office a staff capacity, specifically a service staff function, as opposed to the typical advisory role, to provide support efforts to the coordination activity decentralized with the instructional branch of the college. Under a plan of this type, the central staff office would assist in the identification of employers willing to participate in the program, provide for the development of procedural aspects of the program's operation, coordinate with major areas of institutional adminstration, provide a system for form and paperwork flows, assist in directing new students uncertain of their aims to guidance personnel in student services; given adequate staff support, this office could also meet with and assign students interested in cooperative education to instructor-coordinators (as proposed in Chapter Two). There are obviously many variations of services that a central staff could supply to instructor-coordinators in the field.

Advisory Committee Structures

The special role of the primary cooperative education partners—that is, the employer, the instructor, and the coordinator—will be discussed in the following chapter. In the remainder of this chapter a second major organizational thrust will be examined: the advisory committees. Before examining the authority relationships between the advisory committees and cooperative education administration, consider the alternative forms of advisory committees to be found in community colleges: a central coordinating advisory committee; a steering committee; a program advisory committee; a cooperative education advisory committee; a cooperative education task force committee.

The central coordinating advisory committee usually consists of twenty to forty of the community's most influential leaders, representing journalism, medicine, science, the military, agriculture, industry, education, commerce, urban government, and the social professions. This group, which effectively represents the community's power structure, along with the upper administrative hierarchy of the college, has as its purpose the identification of broad areas of educational need in the immediate community. While this advisory committee's primary mission is to direct the college into new program areas, it can also be an agent for changing the existing bureaucratic structure in the community. For example, the committee might lay down new policy concerning the employment of two-year graduates, or it might act as a stimulus to the community's acceptance of cooperative education. Sinclair Community College in Dayton, Ohio, successfully operates such an advisory committee.

As broad educational needs are identified by the central committee, persons known to possess expertise in the specific areas of need are organized into a steering committee; their function is to advise college personnel on the precise nature and extent of the need for an associate degree program, or perhaps a certificate program, in the immediate community. (Some authorities see the steering committee as having the function of what is referred to in this text as a central coordinating advisory committee with up to 25 members.) Obviously the community college's decision to serve this educational need is influenced by other factors, including community surveys and contacts with community professional and trade groups knowledgeable about the area. The college's commitment to a cooperative education program should be stressed to these groups so that they may carefully appraise the feasibility of offering such a program, besides determining whether there is a need for it locally. The group dissolves upon a "go" or "no-go" recommendation to the college. If it is decided to offer a new program, a program advisory committee should be appointed. (See Mason and Haines, 1972, pp. 150 and 264, for an excellent discussion of advisory committees.)

The composition of the program advisory committee is

usually six to twelve members who represent appropriate employer-employee groups at various management levels, labor unions, students, and representatives of related community and professional organizations. After the program is fully underway, two to three meetings per year may satisfactorily deal with questions of program operation.

This committee is capable of making several contributions: helping develop the cooperative education program, communicating the values of the program to the community, identifying suitable jobs for students, acting as liaison between the college and the community, providing resource speakers and occupational data concerning the area, developing standards for measuring work and study performance, contributing their combined expertise to the solution of program problems, projecting manpower needs, and evaluating the program's success in achieving its objectives. A study of advisory committees reported by Melvin Barlow reveals that of 33 programs offered in 18 community colleges, 23 or 70 percent had an advisory committee. Of the 23 committees approximately half had a size of ten to twelve members. Approximately half of those advisory committees met twice a year, and when the colleges were asked how active their committees were, 26 percent responded "very active and strong," 22 percent "very active," 34 percent "active," 9 percent "fair," and 9 percent "weak" (Barlow, 1963, pp. 17–21).

The program advisory committee is crucial to the success of individual programs. Typically, community colleges have advisory committees for each of their occupational program areas. This practice is excellent and should be continued, but as cooperative education becomes truly comprehensive and an integral part of all college curriculums, it is recommended that programs in fine arts, humanities, social work, and the whole breadth of general education and university parallel curriculums have their own advisory structures. Such curriculum areas as English and mathematics, which are crucial to all programs but for which there is no equivalent two-year program, can similarly benefit from seasoned professionals representing those respective disciplines and organized into a college advisory committee.

The fourth advisory committee is of particular significance to the operation of the cooperative education program; it is the cooperative education advisory committee. The exemplary cooperative education program at the Borough of Manhattan Community College under the direction of Edward Lewis employs an excellent committee of this sort. This committee, called the Advisory Council on Cooperative Education, was in 1970 chaired by Mrs. G. G. Michelson, a vice-president of Macy's. This committee is made up of approximately fifty leaders from various occupational areas of New York life, and they meet periodically to give direction to the College's cooperative education program. An unusual feature of the Manhattan Community College's organization is that they have no formal program advisory committees—instead, the cooperative education advisory committee breaks into smaller groups, representing program areas, to deal with specific problems as they develop. The scope of the authority of this advisory committee structure is suggested in a speech delivered by Mrs. Michelson: "Our council is composed of fifty outstanding representatives of business, government, and labor organizations. . . . Our members work on committees which meet and function, especially when there are problems in the fields of accounting, advertising, data processing, marketing, secretarial science. We rely on them for suggestions on keeping the curriculum up to date and to help the staff secure internship opportunities. . . . Certainly, a most important function of the advisory committee members is to spread the word about the value and importance of cooperative education throughout the business community. . . . On a personal and more selfish note, through the Advisory Council, members learn first-hand about the concerns of young college people as well as the problems of our educators in dealing with these concerns. . . . In a world where communication is instant, and frequently futile, the advisory council appears to be an instrument through which effective communication between the institution, the student, and the business community can be achieved" (Michelson, 1970, pp. 19–20).

Here are some recommendations for developing an advisory committee (D. Billings, 1970, pp. 86–87): (1) Be assured that members understand their duties. (2) Include various levels (people on the actual job, and on supervisory and managerial levels). (3) Stagger terms in office, rotate members, and review makeup of the committee according to priority of objectives. (4) Include some employees as well as employers. (5) Add persons with hiring capabilities. (6) Include representatives of labor and manpower groups. (7) Add persons with access to media. (8) Include college trained personnel. (9) Represent all sizes of business and industry. (10) Organize and regularly schedule meetings.

The fifth form of advisory committee is called the cooperative education task force, and its membership includes a representative sampling of college personnel, including cooperative coordinators, guidance counselors, representatives of various administrative functions, faculty, and, of special importance, students. The group may consist of from ten to twenty members and may meet three to four times a year. The purpose of the committee is to achieve a better understanding of cooperative education and a unification of diverse college elements in the achievement of its objectives. Inputs from this committee will serve to suggest ways to strengthen the bond between work and study, to improve work study curriculum plans, to promote the cooperative education concept among all persons connected with the college, to generate information on ways to improve operational procedure, to suggest possible employers, and to make the cooperative education program as responsive as possible to the needs of students.

It is not recommended that a college commit itself to all six variations of committees; this presentation was designed to expose the various nuances of advisory committee operation. A cooperative education advisory committee that is closely allied with program advisory committees, and represents all college instructional areas, is the heart of an advisory system that would further the objectives of the community college cooperative education program. The larger cooperative education advisory committee could take on the complexion and responsibilities of the central coordinating advisory committee, reducing the overlap of these two bodies while clearly establishing the institution's commitment to cooperative education.

Regardless of the ultimate advisory committee structure, it is recommended that membership extend from one to three years, based on a staggered term of office and a rotating membership arrangement. Several years of participation on the advisory committee from a variety of persons with expertise in this area allows an opportunity for a quantatively greater number of community inputs, a wider participation of community leaders, and a qualitatively superior advisory process. A formal invitation to membership in an advisory committee should come from the president of the college, or from its board of trustees. This lends prestige to the appointment and clarifies the committee's authority. Advisory committees should elect officers—most desirably, a president, a vice-president, and a recording secretary. College representatives on the committee usually sit in an ex officio capacity (Mason and Haines, 1972, p. 150), but some committees have successfully used college personnel as members and even as chairmen of the committee. Meetings should be held periodically throughout the school year; it is critical that these meetings be structured around meaningful issues clearly specified in an agenda, and that all members of the committee be encouraged to participate fully.

★★★★★★★★★★★★★ 6 ★★★★★★★★★★★★★
★★★★★★★★★★★★★   ★★★★★★★★★★★★★

The Co-Op Triangle:
Coordinator, Instructor,
Employer

★★★★★★★★★★★★★★★★★★★★★★★★★★★★★★★★★★★★
★★★★★★★★★★★★★★★★★★★★★★★★★★★★★★★★★★★★

The employer, the instructor, and the cooperative coordinator are the key staff persons in the cooperative education program, and in this chapter each role will be examined separately.

The Coordinator

The cooperative education coordinator is portrayed by Charles Seaverns as a college staff member "who is usually a member of the full-time faculty, with academic rank, serves in the multifaceted capacity of placement officer, student personnel counselor, salesman, teacher, administrator, educational recruiter, troubleshooter, disciplinarian, and referral agent" (1970, p. 14; see also Huber, 1971, p. 89). Butler and York (1971) examine the leadership responsibilities of the cooperative coordinator.

The coordinator as an educational planner:
  (1) conducts student interest surveys
  (2) conducts employer availability survey
  (3) writes policies, standards, and agreements
  (4) assists with budget development
  (5) assists with scheduling programs
The coordinator as a public relations specialist:
  (1) engages in promotional activities
  (2) prepares reports and other information releases of interest to the public
The coordinator as an administrator and educator:
  (1) organizes advisory committees and makes certain they are functioning well
  (2) arranges student interviews and placement with approved employers
  (3) assists students to obtain work permits, Social Security cards, and health certificates
  (4) develops student schedules
  (5) coordinates in-school instruction and on-the-job experience
  (6) establishes defined outcomes for the work period in conjunction with the student and employer
  (7) confers with employers at regular intervals and visits students on the job
The coordinator as a counselor:
  (1) confers with students about personal and program problems
  (2) assists students in reviewing career options
The coordinator as an evaluator:
  (1) develops community employment profiles
  (2) determines readiness of students for cooperative program
  (3) determines suitability of employers for cooperative program
  (4) performs continuous planned evaluation of the total program
  (5) conducts follow-up studies of graduates (Butler and York, 1971, pp. 8–9.)

A profile of the "median" two-year college coordinator is provided by Wilson and Barlow. Based on the existing data, he typically handles a student load of approximately fifty students or a median load of roughly twenty to twenty-five in a strictly cooperative vocational education program. (It should be noted that this data reflects coordination that is combined with other functions, for example, administration or teaching as an instructor-coordinator it would not be unusual to find full time coordinators handling 150 students.) The typical coordinator is paid between $11,000 and $13,000 a year; he visits his students on the job at least once a work period; if he is a teacher-coordinator in a two-year college vocational program, he visits his students several times during the work period; he typically holds a masters degree and has several years of work experience; he has probably been employed in a cooperative education position for only a few years. Finally, usual community college practice is to grant cooperative education coordinators faculty rank (Barlow, 1963; Wilson, 1970, 1971, 1972).

What are the attitudinal dimensions of the "median" community-junior college co-op cordinator? A study conducted by Wilson (1969, pp. 49–50) of the priority beliefs of thirty cooperative education staff members at Northeastern University as it related to their students reveals that "sensitivity to student feelings, interest in the student as a person, and a readiness to listen to student problems" were perceived to be most crucial. Wanda Mosbacker suggests that the relatively unsophisticated task of matching student to work position is being replaced by an important new counseling role for the coordinator. She observes: "In order to assist each student to reach the fullest potential within his career area, the total career counseling function has become the major role of the coordinator." The cooperative education cordinator is not seen as a vocational guidance counselor, but rather as a "central force in assisting each student to reach his ultimate objective of preparing himself for a personally satisfying career. . . . The matching functions, in fact, may become more and more the function of the machine, and less and less that of the coordinator." She sees the coordinator performing the role of a "catalyst between the students and their cooperative employers" (Mosbacker, 1969, p. 32).

To suggest that coordination is career or personal counseling alone is to simplify this very complex cooperative function. A whole set of component processes are set into motion by the coordinator. These component activities, the "nitty-gritty" of the cooperative education endeavor will be explored in later chapters. But what are the qualities which identify an outstanding prospective cooperative education coordinator? (1) He should possess competence in guidance and counseling, employer relations, occupational outlook, placement procedures, public relations, administrative practices, employment standards, instructional skills, and competence in enlisting teaching faculty and work supervisors in the student's learning process. (2) Personally, he should have a contemporary appearance, people orientation (over and above a simple task orientation), self-confidence, empathy, strong motivation, organizational and administrative sensitivity, and a friendly, personable style. (3) His educational preparation would ideally include a masters degree (and most desirably in the field of community college and cooperative education). He should have educational awareness and knowledge in the technical areas he coordinates and in professional subjects such as testing, counseling, and coordination, and the teaching-learning process.

Where does one go to find personnel with such credentials? There are several possibilities: existing staff members at the college (faculty or administration); alumni of the college; recent graduates of graduate degree programs (in cooperative education, community college education, vocational education, guidance, administration, or from a professional school, business, engineering, etc., or a liberal arts program, as the position dictates); persons referred by the administration or board of trustees; persons referred by cooperative education conferences; persons who could be pirated from another institution (a questionable ethical practice); and persons working in community organizations.

What is the best educational preparation for a coordinator is an unresolved issue among cooperative education professionals. Certainly, programs specifically designed to prepare cooperative educators (as at Northeastern University) offer significant advantages, but programs in vocational teacher education that stress the role of coordination in vocational program operation (as at Ohio State, Michigan State, and Minnesota) offer a realistic alternative. The view of coordination as a counseling activity (Pratt, 1972, pp. 46–48, and Mosbacker, 1969, pp. 31–32) suggests opportunities for graduate studies in personnel or career counseling, which are offered at many universities. Professional studies in business, public administration, engineering, or one of the health areas could be excellent preparation if the coordinator is to be an adjunct to one of those occupational programs in the community college. The peculiar institutional, curricular, and student patterns of the community college argue the need for a community college component in any coordinator training program. Certainly the programs at U.C.L.A. and Ohio State suggest the kind of training useful to this purpose. A graduate program designed to prepare community college cooperative education coordinators ought to provide for internships in community college cooperative education programs in conjunction with a seminar on the history, philosophy, and development of cooperative education and the community college.

But W. D. Bostwick's warning (1972, p. 49) should be heeded: "Mere attainment of a particular level or receipt of an academic degree in a specific discipline will not assure the coordinator's success or failure in obtaining challenging and popular job assignments, especially when the economy is operating at a low ebb. Similarly, a specific number of years of industrial work experience does little to insure the coordinator's ability to relate to the changing needs of students and their environment."

To the extent that cooperative education is decentralized in the community college, division chairmen will have a voice in, or sometimes full responsibility for, the hiring of cooperative coordinators. In this case the respective chairman will undoubtedly be influenced by work and educational experiences directly supportive of the area of instructional responsibility. Centralized programs that are staffed by a cooperative administrator would be especially receptive to prospective coordinators having a guidance expertise as well as a work orientation.

La Guardia Community College's cooperative education program, under the capable direction of Harry Heineman, has successfully used coordinators with a wide range of work experiences, educational preparations, ages, life styles, and personalities. For example, an engineer by training and experience, whose appearance is very conventional, works side by side with a long-haired, "hip" coordinator, who has developed a special rapport with students and has set a record for the most work positions pioneered by any staff member in his first year of work.

The Employer

There is little doubt that the cooperative employer (whether he offers wages or unpaid learning experience)' is a key ingredient in cooperative education, but the mere fact that he is willing to employ students says nothing about the quality of his contribution. The benefits accruing to the employing firm are major inducements for it to join the co-op education partnership, but it is the achievement of the educational objectives of the program that must be the central concern of the employer and the college.

A distinction should be made at this point between the employer and the supervisor or training sponsor. Because of differences in employment situations, employer and supervisor roles are not easily differentiated. A typical situation in a medium-sized or large firm would find the employer establishing broad employment qualifications, interviewing, selecting students, planning future cooperative partnerships, placing students, assigning training sponsors or supervisors to the student, communicating the values of cooperative education and procedural arrangements to the supervisor, and assisting with job counseling and orientation. The supervisor who reports to the employer works closely with the student and aids him in learning to perform in his area of responsibility. The college coordinator and the company supervisor are in close touch throughout the student's training period. The specification of defined outcomes for the student (see Chapter Eight)', and the evaluation of them, may be performed by the supervisor or employer, but it is typically done by the supervisor; similarly, if the college uses a student evaluation form in lieu of the defined outcomes approach, the supervisor frequently is asked to complete it. In smaller firms, the employer doubles as the student's supervisor.

From here on, all references to the employer should be assumed to include the training sponsor relationship to the student. Basically, the tasks of the cooperating employer can be reduced to three essential elements: providing the necessary background and knowledge for the student to perform his task efficiently (participating in the definition of learning objectives); supervising the cooperative student during his work period; and evaluating the student's accomplishments.

To the completion of these tasks, certain employer qualities are especially relevant. Empathy is a particularly desirable attribute, for an employer can best contribute to student growth if he is sensitive to the student's needs for independence, individuality, pride, and a sense of belonging and acomplishment. Because the employer performs a kind of teaching function, he should possess the ability to communicate clearly and concisely, tactfully criticizing the student's performance, and willingly answering all questions. Ideally, he should provide encouragement and reward for the student as he grasps the fundamentals of the job and applies classroom principles.

Careful evaluation of the employer as a training sponsor is essential. Some employers simply do not contribute to student growth or the achievement of program objectives, and in these cases the coordinator should intervene to restructure the learning situation. The evaluative procedure should consider the employer's abilities to be sensitive to student needs; to creatively communicate job training to the student, given his learning capability; to work with the coordinator in planning work outcomes and gearing experience to the student's occupational or personal objectives; to demonstrate interest in the student and in the achievement of his educational goals; to perform in a socially responsible manner so as to elicit respect and a professional sensitivity from the student.

The Cooperative Education Association in 1970 offered guidelines for employers entering into a partnership with a college in a cooperative education program. Here are those guidelines:

(1) A realization on the part of the employer that cooperative education is first and foremost an educational program integrated with practical experience. From an educational viewpoint, the employer should give considerable importance to the meshing of particular academic experiences with practical factors at the working site; a series

of coordinated experiences for the student as he returns to the employer in succeeding employment periods; the placing of the student in those areas of employment which will be most conducive to the learning process; and the consideration of the long-range objectives of both the student and the employer.

(2) A genuine interest in integrating and developing the cooperative student as a 'team member' in the organization.

(3) A top-level mangement commitment that the cooperative education program will be an important program in the personal development of the corporation.

(4) The appointment of a well-qualified company coordinator who understands and is in agreement with the objectives of cooperative education. He must have a good knowledge of the colleges and universities with which he will be working and of their academic programs. He should have a recognized position that will enable him to develop the program throughout the corporation.

(5) Close attention to the supervisor of cooperative students, with emphasis on placing the students under supervisors who can see their roles as "educators" as well as supervisors.

(6) Establishment of a separate budget for salaries paid to cooperative students, enabling the student to be placed in any appropriate department. This avoids the imposition on normal operating budgets and tends to be a financial safeguard for the program.

(7) A philosophy within the organization that the program will be sustained to a reasonable degree through normal fluctuations in economic conditions.

(8) A well-planned series of experiences for the student, creating an attractive and viable program which will cause a favorable reaction and contribute to his personal development.

(9) The payment of a salary to the student which is fair and competitive.

(10) While the granting of fringe benefits is not a

*requirement for participation in a cooperative program, it
is desirable to give the student as many advantages as possible. The more 'he looks like' a permanent employee, the
more likely he is to think in terms of permanent association
with the employer.* [*Hunt and Knowles,* Handbook of Cooperative Education, *1971, p. 172.*]

D. Keith Lupton, in discussing the role of the employer,
notes that his role is "so very important that a failure here can be as
effective (or more so) in disrupting a successful program as a failure
on the part of students or educators" (1969, p. 52). Lupton gives
consideration to seven phases of the cooperating employer function;
each of these is briefly abstracted in the following (1969, pp. 52–
56):

(1) The employer should be involved in the planning so as
to provide a sequence of planned activities (job rotation); a pay
schedule which is sufficiently motivating; authority relationships to
carry out the supervision of students; commitment to the accomplishment of the cooperative education program's objectives; and
an effective communications system to avoid problems.

(2) A successful working relationship between college, student, and employer hinges on the employer's provision of clear
information about the kind of student wanted; his rapid consideration of the student and a decision to accept or reject the student;
and communications that are made directly to the cooperative coordinator.

(3) A student orientation process hinges on the employer's
provision of an introduction to key organizational personnel; of
encouragement to the student to discuss his cooperative program
with his supervisor; and of information as to the firm's function and
in particular the student's role in the organization.

(4) The student supervision process hinges on the employer's
provision of authority for students commensurate with work requirements and program objectives (educational values for students); a feedback system to determine student performance;
regular communication with the coordinator about the student's
progress; and regular meetings with the student to review his performance.

(5) The student evaluation process hinges on the employer's provision of an honest, objective evaluation, and signatures of all those taking part in the evaluation.

(6) Extracurricular assistance hinges on the employer's provision of suggestions for outside reading; special company services (subscription to house organ, tickets to special events, etc.); and a means for interaction between co-op students working at the firm.

(7) Cooperative education professionalism hinges on the employer's attendance at cooperative education conferences; publication of his experiences with cooperative education, and occasional employment of community college faculty members.

Wallace (1970, pp. 25–26) refers to a study which was made by Cushman of cooperative vocational education at the secondary level, but which has implications for community college educators. Cushman contrasts expectations of students with expectations of employers. He found that students expected specific training for an occupation; academic credit for the work experience; varied and interesting work assignments; pleasant, fair, and helpful supervision; at least the minimum wage; and experience leading to further training.

The expectations of employers were quite different; they expected the students to have the ability to perform a variety of tasks, good work habits, and desirable personal attributes. They wanted the school to provide specific occupational training, effective coordination, and solutions to problems that might arise.

Butler and York, commenting on the Cushman study, note that it points out the most critical potential defect of cooperative education: "Employers viewed the student essentially as a part time worker. . . . Students expected the experience to have educational significance" (1971, p. 12).

Employer participation and involvement is absolutely essential to the achievement of program objectives. Wallace (1970, p. 26) recommends that training sponsors should be selected from those "who *expect* to sacrifice the usual productivity for educational significance, and who show a willingness to utilize their production as a vehicle for education."

Employer development is crucial, and special sessions held on campus or at the employment site can be useful in setting forth the philosophy and purposes of the program. Merritt College in Oakland, California, is one example of the kind of sponsor development which is possible in community college cooperative education programs. In April 1972, Merritt conducted a cooperative education meeting with students, college personnel, and employers. Minutes from the meeting indicated that an important emphasis of the session was "the goals and needs of the cooperative education program as seen from the perspective of these three groups." This sort of involvement of employers is useful for creating a stronger employer identification with the college's program while serving to upgrade or develop employer practices as they relate to the student (Schuetz, April 28, 1972).

Warren Meyer, in urging sponsor development notes that occupational competence does not insure teaching competence. Employers, he writes, "often tend to assume that the learner can perform a task after being told and shown once how it should be done." He recommends a sponsor development program which focuses on four important teaching tasks: preparing the learner, presenting the material, applying the learning, and checking on learning (1969, pp. 67–68).

The Instructor

Faculty members have a changed role in a cooperative education community college. A new perspective is required in classroom teaching to effectively integrate work with study. When seeking staff members, community college administrators ought to explain the special nontraditional role of the instructor in the cooperating college and try to assess the willingness of the candidate to perform such a role. One plan advocated in these pages decentralized coordination to the faculty level, creating the function of instructor-coordinator in most instructional areas (not just in the occupational curriculums); this plan further complicates the staffing problem because two very different kinds of expertise are necessary to effectively perform both teaching and coordination functions. The remainder of this chapter will examine the unique position of the teaching function alone.

The Wilson and Lyons study revealed that faculties who are

not encouraged to participate in cooperative education planning suffer a lack of understanding about what the program philosophy and objectives are. Faculty members may not take advantage of the opportunity to deal with both study and work experiences in class. Wilson and Lyons state (1961, p. 11): "We recommend that, in initiating a plan of cooperative education, the faculty be intimately involved in planning, particularly as it relates to their own teaching, and that after the program is established there be continuous or periodic participation by the faculty in planning and coordination so that they will have a more adequate understanding of the potential and the problems to guide their own teaching."

To oversimplify somewhat, it could be argued that faculty members have three responses to the cooperative education modification of the college's programs: to support such a change enthusiastically, creatively adapting their instructional approaches to the new system; to accept the program passively, without a clear sense of its implications for classroom instruction; or to actively disapprove of cooperative education and its intrusions on program, curriculum, or course offerings. The second response often occurs when community colleges adopting cooperative programs do little to explain the special relevance of cooperative education to their faculty members. To fail to establish effective communications, or, worse, to decide to undertake a cooperative education program without the participation of faculty, makes the third response a real possibility. Asa Knowles states (1971, pp. 228–229): "One of the difficulties encountered in cooperative education programs over the years has been the lack of support, and at times outright hostility, toward the system itself on the part of some faculty members." This hostility has manifested itself in open encouragement of students not to participate in the program (when it is optional). More than one institution has experienced morale problems due to disagreements and faculty antagonism toward cooperative education.

To overcome this obstacle, effective communications coupled with faculty participation are imperative. The task force advisory committee discussed in the previous chapter is an excellent vehicle for achieving a limited faculty involvement. In-training faculty programs and orientation sessions should be regular endeavors, and the regular faculty should be encouraged to visit with the cooperative staff in their meetings and attend cooperative education conferences. The faculty member needs to be recognized as an invaluable resource in maximizing the cooperative education experience, and to this end he should be encouraged to participate in giving perspective and direction to the program.

An additional problem needs recognition. Ideological and philosophical stances of faculty members sometimes impede program success. Specifically, faculty members in general education and university parallel areas are sometimes prone to resist what they see as the "vocationalizing" of their programs. The stereotype of cooperative education as vocational education must be attacked by detailed explanations of its advantages to non-occupational faculty members. It must be made clear that cooperative education can contribute to the student's personal development by offering opportunities to apply concepts and principles studied in liberal arts curriculums. Knowles, commenting on the "less receptive" response of some liberal arts educators, notes: "This problem is rapidly becoming minimized—particularly since direct connections between the work and study aspects of the educational program are being deemphasized, especially in the humanities and social sciences. In nontechnical areas, emphasis is often on the human development of the student as an individual" (1971, pp. 229–230).

The experience of one faculty member in a cooperative education college suggests another kind of resistance. Leonard E. Plachta, chairman of the accounting department at the University of Detroit, has written (1969, p. 19): "The typical professor is not eager to have others, especially non-teachers, participate in the education of his students. . . . The co-op student's return to the classroom after a work period can be a disquieting factor in the classroom. The co-op student, now exposed to the 'real' world, is in a better position to question, and to argue with the professor." Plachta sees this as "healthy and beneficial," but also as "a possible threat to the teacher who is not accustomed to being questioned."

Interestingly enough, there is some indication that faculty members get "higher marks" from cooperative education students than from regular students. Lentz and Seligsohn report on a comparison between co-op and regular students on eleven different scales and note that the only significant difference ($P < .05$) between the two groups was on the "satisfaction with faculty" scale, where the co-op students expressed a greater satisfaction with the teaching staff (1968, p. 30).

J. Dudley Dawson writes, "The academic faculty should attempt to relate the content and style of their teaching to whatever work experience the students have had or will have in the future." Because of the varying objectives typical of the community college student body, faculty members need to be alert to these differences and should "improvise the means of making cooperative education serve the personal, career, and scholastic needs of the students." Dawson goes on to give illustrations of the ways in which work experiences can complement study. In technology or occupational courses, "the classroom dialogue can act as a motivator for students looking forward to field applications, or as an opportunity for comparing theory being discussed in the classroom with the practice students can report from previous job experiences." He continues, "in courses like psychology, sociology, political science, history, and religion, instructors can stimulate students, regardless of the kind of job on which they may be placed, to test out ideas and principles being advanced by observing how they check out in reality." In addition, "The cooperative work reports, which all students write each job period, offer unique opportunities for developing good writing skills. Arrangements could be readily made so that cooperative work reports would become an integral part of every student's instruction in English composition" (Dawson, 1972, pp. 3–5).

On balance, the potential for maximizing educational values of the cooperative program lies to an important extent with faculty members. A truly viable integration of work and study experience requires a changed perspective for faculty members, and a new conception of faculty identity. That new identity for the faculty member might be that of an "experiential integrator."

An "experiential integrator" plans every part of his instructional effort with his student's work experience in mind. He assumes the responsibility for knowing about the current job placements of his students; he designs instructional ingredients so as to relate to the breadth of these experiences; he plans his class sessions to allow time for student discussion of work experiences related to class themes; he prepares examinations for his class which allow students to make relationships between work and study; he emphasizes key variables that students ought to watch for during work periods; he assigns term papers which ask that students integrate important aspects of their work with the thesis of their reports; and he prepares instructional objectives for his course which require students to consider work and study relationships. The faculty member becomes an active participant in the cooperative education program. The strategic aspect of his role in the cooperative education program must be discussed in faculty meetings, orientation programs, college-sponsored in-service training programs, and regional workshops. Only in these ways can "experiential integration" become a reality in the classroom.

★★★★★★★★★★★★★★ 7 ★★★★★★★★★★★★★★
★★★★★★★★★★★★★★ ★★★★★★★★★★★★★★

Obtaining, Scheduling, and Promoting Work Experience

★★★★★★★★★★★★★★★★★★★★★★★★★★★★★★★★★★
★★★★★★★★★★★★★★★★★★★★★★★★★★★★★★★★★★

A critical ingredient of the work experience aspect of the community college cooperative education program is the student's placement. The care with which cooperative education placements are selected and developed is extremely important to program success. Mason and Haines point out that a student job should be selected "primarily as a training medium rather than merely as an opportunity for remunerative employment for the student or for an employer to obtain part time help" (1972, p. 219). A guiding principle in selecting work positions is that the coordinator be certain that the employer supports the educational goals of the program.

Cooperating employers should be chosen to serve the needs of students attending the community college. For example, a community college enrolling a heavily career-oriented student population would select a different mix of work positions than a college with a predominantly university transfer program. The former would probably emphasize specific career categories in middle management and semi-professional fields (for example, accounting, electrical engineering, and nursing) and would gear its program toward technical skill development, while the latter would deemphasize particular occupational categories and would concentrate on opportunities for personal development and exploration. More specifically, the pioneering of training positions ought to progress from a projection of student needs to a plan for suitably approaching possible cooperating employers. Consideration should be given to the breadth of student needs, including geographic proximity of the employment site to the student's home.

Dawson points out that approximately 70 percent of community college students hold part-time employment (1971, p. 11); these part-time jobs can occasionally be developed into cooperative education training opportunities, when the work is related to the student's educational objective and the conditions of an educationally relevant work situation can be justified. Students may be persistent about remaining in the positions they have held before entering the college, but the cooperative education staff should stress the educational aspects of the program, evaluating the work in light of the student's needs.

Seaverns (1970, p. 55) recommends the following sources of information for use in planning cooperative education work positions:

(1) United States Census Report. *Invaluable indicator of the industrial and occupational distribution of the gainfully employed and unemployed in given geographic areas as well as a description of population trends.*

(2) Help wanted advertisements. *Good source of leads for potential cooperative employment.*

(3) Special news items. *Information about new organizations being formed, branch offices being opened, and promotions and changes of personnel being made.*

(4) Classified telephone directory. *An indication of*

the number and variety of business activities in the community.

(5) Trade and association journals. *Information pertaining to the general situation in a specific vocational area.*

(6) Business and product directories. *Detailed lists of companies, products, and personnel in different geographic locations.*

Seaverns suggests (pp. 36–37) that small, family operated firms be avoided because of nepotism; he adds that firms with high personnel turnover rates usually have more job openings than firms with stable employment, and that larger companies are more predisposed to participation in a program because of their more enlightened outlook toward training programs. On balance, some small firms make excellent training sites, because students are exposed to the breadth of company operations and proprietors of these firms are sometimes able to offer close and special attention to students, which is not always obtainable in large and impersonal organizations. Similarly, while firms with high manpower turnover may be prime targets for student placement, the disadvantage of instability and impermanence of positions must be considered.

Assurance also needs to be given that the employer will provide adequate supervision by assigning a sponsor for the student to oversee his work, answer questions, and direct his activities on the job. Adequate supervision is crucial to the educational validity of the program. The reasonable probability that work sites will be available on a continuing basis is important to program continuity. Some employers, while supportive of the educational purposes of the program, may agree to provide short-term or seasonal jobs without any intention of giving long-term cooperation. This is not always undesirable, and in some colleges such an arrangement can be planned so as to offer advantages for all concerned. However, if the coordinator is not aware of this, students who are placed on the job will be penalized by the on-again, off-again nature of the experience. The employer should be encouraged to discuss his objectives for participating in the program, and if it is determined that seasonal employment demands are an influencing factor, then the college might arrange for a limited or special alternation pattern. Grahm Junior College in Boston is an excellent illustration; their retailing students co-op only during the holiday rush between Thanksgiving and Christmas, and their hotel-motel students complete the work experience portion of their program during the summer. This kind of non-traditional scheduling can meet employers' as well as students' needs (Grahm Junior College, 1971–1972).

The quality of the training site needs to be carefully evaluated. Does the job offer sufficient challenge and responsibility to foster the achievement of the educational aims of the student, or is it menial work allowing only limited opportunities for learning? However, certain cooperative positions, while appearing to be overly routine, could in fact be useful for a variety of reasons, such as providing an opportunity for important interpersonal interactions, or an opportunity to work for or observe an especially gifted manager. An effective coordinator will alert the student to these potential learning situations, while being completely honest about the nature of the assignment. The adequacy and up-to-date condition of facilities and equipment should be assured; here the argument can be forcefully made that the task of verifying the educational validity of the work position is best performed by a coordinator who possesses the necessary expertise and understanding of the occupation to enable him to make a fair judgment.

Working conditions should be judged healthful and completely above-board, and socially irresponsible or unethical employers should not be encouraged to participate in the program. Wages and fringe benefits should be in line with those being paid for similar work in other institutions. The presence of a union and its associated standards and practices should be investigated to make certain that it does not intrude upon cooperative program operations. Communications with union leaders and the encouragement of their participation on the advisory committee is an important coordination tactic, especially in those industries where unions have important influence.

It is essential that the employer enhance the learning situation by permitting visitations, meeting with the coordinator and student to establish designated outcomes for the work experience, filling out necessary forms, and evaluating the student's performance in light of the defined objectives (Chapter Eight). In setting instructional objectives, the employer must recognize the student's capacity and abilities so as to challenge him sufficiently but not establish unrealistic goals. The employer's human relations and educational sensitivity should be ascertained, and employers insensitive in this regard might better be excluded from the program. The employer's hiring, rotation, advancement, and dismissal practices should be consistent with the program's aims, and the opportunity for varied work experiences should be provided throughout the student's work experience.

It is obvious that the selection of training positions is not a simple task involving the mere approval of an employer to take on part-time community college students to satisfy his employment needs. It is not college placement, nor is it the federally funded work-study type of student employment (although this can be administered to achieve co-op education standards). A viable cooperative education program requires that the coordination activity carefully provide for meaningful work experience opportunities that have educational relevance to the student's objectives with specifically designated and measurable learning outcomes. Cooperative education requires a special network of responsibilities linking employer, college, and student, and some community colleges feel that because of the educational objectives of the program and the relationship between the three parties an employment contract should be required. Wilson notes that about 37 percent of the collegiate programs in his survey have a student employment contract, but not all programs using a contract require all three parties to sign (1971, p. 48). Some colleges argue that a formal contract may suggest a sense of distrust and be an overly rigid requirement in an enterprise that must ultimately rely on the best intentions of all participating parties. Some employers simply wish to avoid the regulation of such a contract. However, Dopp and Nicholson (p. 11) advocate a training agreement which clearly specifies the responsibilities of employer, student, and college. They suggest that the following areas be included in the agreement:

(1) The duties of the student.

(2) The number of hours the student is to spend on the job.

(3) The responsibilities of the student in such matters as: (a) notifying the employer in case of unavoidable absence; (b) observing safety rules; (c) observing business etiquette; (d) cooperating with his supervisor; (e) attending classes regularly.

(4) The responsibilities of the employer for: (a) training and supervising the student; (b) providing the student with a variety of learning experiences; (c) recording the student's attendance and keeping the instructor-coordinator informed as to his conduct on the job and his progress in learning on the job; (d) obeying wage and hour laws and safety regulations.

(5) The responsibilities of the college for: (a) providing overall supervision and coordination of the program; (b) providing related instruction; (c) selecting capable students who will profit from the program.

Other points which may be covered in the training agreement include the addresses and telephone numbers of all participating parties, the beginning and ending dates of the work experience period, the average number of hours to be worked, the student's rate of pay, conditions justifying a change in the assignment of a student, conditions for terminating the training agreement, the student's pledge to remain with the employer for the duration of the period, and the signatures of all parties involved. The model program presented in Chapter Two combines the training agreement with the statement of defined outcomes, which specifies the learning objectives for the period into a single form (see Exhibit A). This approach is recommended as being an especially effective technique for commiting all parties to the educational parameters of the program and especially to the notion of achieving specified learning objectives. The experience of the California community college cooperative education experiment, with over 4000 students a year using a variation on such a plan, gives an indication of its workability.

Traditionally, the heart of cooperative education, especially the vocational style of cooperative education, is what is called a training plan. Mason and Haines and a long list of vocational educators have advocated step by step sequencing of learning activities which the college and employer will provide in order to develop skills, attitudes, and abilities needed for a successful career in the student's field of career interest (Mason and Haines, 1972, pp. 221–223). Such a written plan is workable in vocational programs on the secondary school level, where the teacher-coordinator has one group of students for a full year and teaches most of their vocational courses, but it is practically impossible to apply at the community college, given the alternating block type of cooperative education and the probable variations and changes in the scheduling of course work. In the absence of a training plan, the cooperative coordinator has the special responsibility to stay in close touch with the employer and student to ascertain the requirements of the work and the desirability of certain course sequences progressing in relationship to the increasing responsibilities of the student worker. The use of the defined outcomes approach, in which the employer, coordinator, and student meet to establish learning objectives, allows an opportunity to build into the objectives certain aspects of classroom theory and to decide upon a pattern of course sequencing that best complements the work experience part of the student's program.

The selection of training sites and the assurance of an educational contribution to the student's objectives are the logical first steps in the cultivation of work positions, but the process should not stop there; a continuing development and upgrading of the educational opportunities provided by the employer is required. The development of the training site—or sponsor development, as it is sometimes called—is not an easy task (see Chapter Six). It is facilitated by frequent coordinator visits, but a more effective means of guarding against stagnation and mediocrity is the encouragement of the active participation of employers and their supervisors in the discussion of cooperative education problems. Monthly breakfast or luncheon meetings of work sponsors to discuss operational aspects of the program can add measurably to the continued refinement of the cooperative education program. Such meetings should be planned by the coordinator but conducted by those employers who are especially adept at the task of cooperative education student supervision. Regardless of the technique, efforts should be made to arrange regular meetings with co-op employer groups.

The hard work of employers in guiding and directing students should not go unnoticed. A highly recommended activity is the provision of a "bosses night," at which cooperative students invite their work sponsors to an evening dinner meeting near the end of the school year with selected faculty members and administrators present; the purpose would be to express thanks to the employers for their contribution. A banquet meal, awards to outstanding employers, and a program planned by the cooperative education staff and students could constitute the agenda. Local newspaper and television reporters may be invited to publicize the good works of the cooperating companies. In a comprehensive, mandatory program or in an optional program with a large student enrollment, coordinators representing individual program specializations should organize a "bosses night" for students with similar educational objectives.

Scheduling Work-Study Alternations

Variations of work and study alternations in community colleges are contingent upon a number of factors: the degree of institutional commitment to cooperative education (for example, from one period of study to as many as six periods in some two-year colleges); the institution's philosophical orientation toward career education, general education, or the comprehensive model (some vocational educators favor a half-day plan, while many general cooperative education programs practice an alternating term); its academic calendar (quarter versus trimester versus semester systems); and unusual requirements of employers caused by seasonal changes or other irregularities of operation requiring the combination of work and study periods in unorthodox patterns. To a large extent, institutional philosophy and calendar should determine the plan for integrating work and study components. Nevertheless, the details of several plans, and their respective advantages and disadvantages, will be discussed at a later point in this chapter.

Interestingly enough, the institution's philosophy of vocational education, general education, or some combination of the two dictates a pattern of work and study for cooperative education. Dudley Dawson, in discussing alternation plans, points out, "many of those in vocational cooperative education are on half-day alternation of study and work periods during the academic year. . . . In the more general types of cooperative education, students usually alternate periods of study with periods of employment" (1971, p. 15)'.

The pattern of half-day cooperative education in vocational programs did not occur by chance, for the vocational education philosophy calls for the closest possible relationship between classroom theory and on-the-job training. Work experiences should influence the type and timing of curriculum. Mary Marks, in reference to one kind of vocational education, distributive education, makes these remarks: "In distributive education, however, the sequence of learning activities becomes a matter of occupational urgency. Course content must be arranged psychologically and practically to satisfy requirements of immediate job performance and ultimate career objectives of those enrolled" (Marks, 1963, p. 5).

The half-day and the alternating block plans have achieved wide acceptance and loyal supporters. Both plans are workable under a variety of conditions. For example, Sinclair Community College in Ohio uses both alternating block and half-day plans in their programs, while the California consortium of cooperative education community colleges uses a half-day plan for its university parallel students as well as for its occupational students.

The alternating block plan allows the student to spend a full term at college and the following full term at work. This plan is conditioned on a team or "buddy system," whereby one student is in college and the other is working full-time; the following quarter the students alternate work and study assignments. The alternating block arrangement typically works on a year-round system, so that the employer has the position filled continually and the student is able to complete his degree more rapidly.

However, there are important advantages of the half-day plan. The employer can also use the team approach under this plan so as to continuously cover a full-time job, or if it better meets his needs he can use co-op students for part-time positions. There are advantages to students; the abrupt, on-again, off-again nature of the alternating block plan is replaced by an uninterrupted flow of work and study. The interaction of the two experiences is a matter of daily urgency. Students under this plan do not need to terminate their college friendships and student associations each period, and their personal finances are more easily managed because income is continuously and evenly generated throughout a collegiate career.

Clearly, the alternating block and the half-day plans each offer a particular set of advantages to the cooperative college, the student, and the employer. Numerous other plans, practiced on a more limited scale, combine work and study in more unorthodox patterns. For example, some two-year colleges provide special internships geared to unusual employer needs for student-trainees during summer holidays or for special sales (Easter, Christmas, inventory closeouts). Brown reports (1970, p. 10) that following the recommendation of a regional administrator of a retail chain store, a plan was devised whereby the student begins his cooperative work period with a retail department store during the summer, immediately upon graduation from high school. He has the option of a reduced academic load and employment during the fall term. In February, after the holiday rush, the student returns to full-time study. This plan helps do three things: solve the problem of seasonal reduction of sales staff after the Christmas rush season; increase the low enrollments in community colleges during the spring semester; and attract young people into the retail sales and marketing fields.

Other community colleges offer a one-term-only plan designed to acquaint the student with an occupational area without slowing up his completion of the two-year degree. Some colleges offer this plan as part of an elective sequence from which the student can select work or classroom experiences.

A real problem for community college cooperative educators is the dilemma caused by the lengthening of the student's program. For many community college students, and especially those planning a transfer to a university, time is valuable, and some are inclined to avoid a co-op program in order to complete the degree in two years. In attacking this problem, Sinclair Community College in Ohio set as its objective the requirement of an internship in its new retailing program which is structured within a time frame of two years. Sinclair is on a quarter schedule and typically requires six academic quarters for the completion of an associate degree. The course content of the new retailing program was reduced to five quarters and the work portion of the program was set at three quarters. By using summer quarters (four quarters per year instead of three), the objective of integrating significant work experience opportunities in the program while maintaining a two-year program was achieved.

Cooperative education for evening students is relatively new, but movements in this direction will surely be rapid. The five-college consortium in California is currently offering such a plan, and approximately 45 percent of the over 4,000 students enrolled in cooperative education are in this program (Bennett and Redding, 1972, p. 4). This plan provides a differentiated conception of community college cooperative education tailored specifically to the needs of students who are working full time. The evening or extended-day cooperative education program is conditioned on the presence of an aggressive cooperative staff, a local institutional commitment to the upgrading of its employees, a definable student need, and close cooperation between the three parties. The student benefits by the recognition of his work experience toward degree requirements. The program schedule for students will depend upon the flexibility of employers; some firms feel that it is so valuable that the employee is granted release time during the day, while other institutions prefer that the classes be taken in evening school. Firms working on multiple shifts can be especially adaptable to such a program. An important aspect of this program is the coordinator's close relationship with the employer; this allows defined outcomes to be established, but more important, it permits a job rotation plan to be developed, so that employees can in fact progress toward their career and personal objectives. This program offers the college the potential of expanding its services to a student clientele which heretofore was only incompletely served. The inducement of receiving credit toward a college degree for work experiences is a powerful one. With the exception of Brown (1971, p. 9), little attention in the literature is given to this form of cooperative plan.

The advantages and disadvantages of college calendars are widely debated by cooperative authorities. The typical alternatives are quarter, semester, and trimester plans, but regardless of schedule, many employers need to be assured that the work opportunities they provide for training will be filled on a year-round basis.

The semester plan may or may not include a brief summer session. (Remarks related to the trimester plan also have applicability to the semester plans with a summer session.) This plan without a summer session is sometimes incompatible with the needs of students, employers, or an effective alternation pattern. The trimester plan typically lasts 14 to 15 weeks, the semester plan 16 to 18, and the quarter 10 to 12 weeks. Assuming an alternating block plan, the important arguments for the quarter system are that the student is able to hold a greater variety of jobs, which is particularly important in a two-year college program for students desiring exploration or a variety of personal development experiences, and it is administratively less complicated to implement an alternating block system with two distinct teams of students. Disadvantages of the quarter system are that the student has only a limited time to adapt to the job and that the more frequent alternations serve to increase paperwork, counseling sessions, visitations and so forth.

Assuming an alternating block plan, the trimester system offers the advantage of providing a more thorough familiarization with the work, a reduced administrative responsibility in terms of communication flows and paperwork, and an increased opportunity for improved counseling and more in-depth job visitations. Disadvantages of the trimester are that the student is limited in the breadth or frequency of his work experiences, the summer term is cumbersome to administer, because of student vacation plans, and a neat, tidy alternating block plan is more difficult to schedule. The summer term may be equally difficult to administer under a quarter system because a year-round calendar of course offerings is not provided and students interrupt their studies for vacations. It is desirable that a cooperative community college be a full-time institution operating on a year-round basis.

Decisions about alternating block, half-day, or evening college co-op, and trimester, quarter, or semester calendars ought to be based on conditions such as the nature of local employment conditions, the requirements of cooperating employers, curricular organization, and student preferences. Table 3 below illustrates the eight basic cooperative education alternation patterns suitable for use at a community college. The quarter system calendar is used in these tables, but the trimester plan can be easily adapted to most of these alternation plans.

Table 3

BASIC ALTERNATION PATTERNS, QUARTER SYSTEM

1. THREE-YEAR ALTERNATING BLOCK PLAN

(Six study periods, five work periods, 90 quarter hours in classwork, uses the team approach)

Year	Student	Fall	Winter	Spring	Summer
One	A	Study	Work	Study	Work
	B	Work	Study	Work	Study
Two	A	Study	Work	Study	Work
	B	Work	Study	Work	Study
Three	A	Study	Work	Study	Work
	B	Work	Study	Work	Study

2. TWO-YEAR ALTERNATING BLOCK PLAN

(Five study periods, three work periods, 75–80 quarter hours in classwork, uses the team approach)

Year	Student	Fall	Winter	Spring	Summer
One	A	Study	Study	Work	Study
	B	Study	Study	Study	Work
Two	A	Work	Study	Work	Study
	B	Study	Work	Study	Work

3. THREE-YEAR HALF-TIME PLAN

(Ten combined study-work periods, 90 quarter hours in classwork, may or may not use the team approach)

Year	Student	Fall	Winter	Spring	Summer
One	A	Study Work	Study Work	Study Work	Study Work
Two	A	Study Work	Study Work	Study Work	Study Work
Three	A	Study Work	Study Work		

4. TWO-YEAR HALF-TIME PLAN

(Three study periods, five combined study-work periods, 90 quarter hours in classwork, may or may not use the team approach)

Year	Student	Fall	Winter	Spring	Summer
One	A	Study	Study	Study	Study Work
Two	A	Study Work	Study Work	Study Work	Study Work

5. TRAILING TERM

(Six study periods, one work period, 90 quarter hours in classwork, may or may not use the team approach)

Year	Student	Fall	Winter	Spring	Summer
One	A	Study	Study	Study	Vacation
Two	A	Study	Study	Work	Study

6. RETAILING HOLIDAY SEASON MODEL

(Five study periods, two combined work-study periods, 90 quarter hours in classwork, may or may not use the team approach)

Year	Student	Fall	Winter	Spring	Summer
One	A	Work Study	Study	Study	Vacation
Two	A	Work Study	Study	Study	Study

7. RETAILING EARLY ADMISSION MODEL

(Four study periods, four combined work-study periods, 90 quarter hours in classwork, may or may not use the team approach)

Year	Student	Fall	Winter	Spring	Summer
One	A	Work Study	Work Study	Study	Study
Two	A	Work Study	Work Study	Study	Study

8. SUMMER SPECIAL

(Six study terms, two work periods, 90 quarter hours in classwork, may or may not use the team approach)

Year	Student	Fall	Winter	Spring	Summer
One	A	Study	Study	Study	Work
Two	A	Study	Study	Study	Work

Wilson's study of collegiate cooperative education programs reveals that in two-year colleges 37.8 percent are semester plans, 26.1 percent are quarter, 20.3 percent are half-day, and the remaining programs are variations. The first work period is in the first year in 72 percent of these colleges; 32.4 percent require one to two work periods, 47.9 percent require three to four, and the remainder require five to seven terms of work or some other arrangement (1972, p. 12).

Students transferring to a university upon graduation will be interested in a "linking" cooperative education plan whereby students transfer from a two-year college cooperative program to a four-year college cooperative program in the same area, maintaining continuity of work placements. In Florida, especially, this kind of development is taking place.

Finally, an important consideration is whether to choose a mandatory or an optional program. At present only one community college in the nation has a completely mandatory program, La Guardia Community College in New York. Several junior colleges and technical institutes operate on such a basis; Cincinnati Technical College offers a particularly outstanding example of a program of this type. Collins reports that 9 percent of reporting two-year colleges offer mandatory programs (1971, p. 34). Twenty percent of the two-year colleges in Wilson's survey provide mandatory programs (1972, p. 12). In reality, there are three alternative enrollment patterns in community college cooperative education: mandatory programs for all students; selective mandatory programs with cooperative education required in certain selected program areas; and optional programs whereby students may choose between full-time study or cooperative education. Wilson's study reveals that over a third of the community-junior colleges in his study operate under the third plan and approximately one-fourth of the institutions offer a mix of the three (1972, p. 12).

Dawson comments: "In too many cases cooperative education appears as a fringe program which is opted by a small segment of the student body. Thus the real thrust of its impact on the curriculum and the teaching-learning is at best only fragmentary. . . . When colleges really believe that non-academic experience should become a part of teaching-learning, student self-development, professional preparation, they will incorporate it in the degree requirement" (1971, p. 7).

Cooperative education is clearly not a single pattern of work and study alternation; in practice, many blends of in-class and out-of-class experience are possible. Patterns of alternation are limited only by the curricular organizations of colleges, the needs of students and employers, and the creativity of coordinators. Unusual and varied work-study plans provide new opportunities for administrators uncontaminated by traditional practice and ready to help forge a new style of experimental learning.

Promoting the Cooperative Program

It is useful to think in terms of three broad target groups, or clienteles, for community college cooperative education—employers, members of the community, and students. Promotion efforts to any one sector to the exclusion of any other can result in a less than adequate network of needs recognition for the program. Each of these groups serves to stimulate needs in the others, which can ultimately result in a wide base of positive interest in a cooperative education program. These clienteles can be further segmented. For example, the needs of employers vary greatly from public to private sectors, from large corporations to smaller sole proprietorships, and from functional area to functional area (for example, from marketing to finance to production). Similarly, student needs differ according to a wide set of demographic characteristics (sex, age, occupation, race, socioeconomic background, and so forth). A simple illustration will serve to make this point. Middle class youth might best be attracted to a cooperative program if stress were laid on such educational values as social relevance, career exploration, innovation in education or the potential for new interpersonal encounters. Disadvantaged and minority youth could be encouraged to enroll by the promise of financial reward and the ability to penetrate the mainstream of community life, whereas adults currently employed could see the program as a means of advancement in a career area. The choice of the appeals to be used should depend upon the target clientele.

In Chapter Two a plea was made for a student orientation as opposed to a process orientation, and the implications of this are very important in promoting a community college cooperative education program. One implication is that presenting details of program operation should be made subordinate to presenting the need-satisfying qualities of the program. Certainly the student needs to be familiar with certain procedural aspects of the program, but each program should be described in ways that emphasize its own particular "need-fulfilling potentials" and not in ways that reveal a traditional preoccupation with calendar and schedule, responsibilities of students, and evaluation criteria.

To put it another way, an important distinction can be made between the features of cooperative education and the benefits to be derived from it, and it is the benefits that should be emphasized in promotion. The features of community college cooperative education include the partnership of employer and college, a pattern of alternating work and study periods, and a unique coordination role for community college administrators, to suggest a few; these are of crucial interest to administrators, but not to prospective students. The benefits to be derived from the program vary according to the target clientele. For students, the chief benefits are opportunities to apply classroom principles in real world situations, to try out or explore occupational fields, to observe first-hand societal, technological, and occupational conditions of the community, and to make extra money. (Over $200 million was earned by cooperative students in 1970–1971. Tyler in Knowles' *Handbook*, 1971, p. 21). Benefits for employers include a supply of enthusiastic students with learning as their primary goal, an opportunity for meeting the community's social responsibilities to its young people, and a means of supplying manpower needs for the future. Benefits for the community include having a new means of speeding the movement of poor and disadvantaged persons into the community's mainstream, a source for supplying occupational needs of community institutions, and a program that will promote a closer relationship between "town and gown."

Butler and York state that cooperative education ought to emphasize the expectations that target clienteles have for the program. They cite Cushman's 1967 study of student and employer expectations, and they suggest that promotion emphasize the following expectations (1971, pp. 11–12). For students: "educational values; specific training for an occupation; academic credit; varied and interesting assignments; supervision that is pleasant, fair, and helpful; at least the minimum wage; opportunities for further training." For employers, the expectations are: "continual placement of students at a single task so as to contribute to the firm's productivity; involvement in the selection of students; provision of students with good work habits and desirable personal attributes; students who are willing to perform a variety of tasks; the college's provision of specific occupational training; the teacher-coordinator's provision of effective coordination and trouble-shooting." However, the tenor of the message directed to employers must clarify the educational implications of the program. Serious tension between employer and college can result if the firm decides to participate in the program only to solve an employment problem and is later confronted by the college about the quality of its educational service.

Broadly speaking, the objectives of promotion are to inform or persuade. Efforts at persuasion have traditionally been discouraged in higher education as somewhat unprofessional, but low pressure, subtle persuasion couched in language suggestive of social service and scholarly pursuits is now finding wider acceptance. Informational promotion is entirely useful given a totally new and widely unfamiliar program. In reality, informational and persuasive promotions can be difficult to distinguish, and effective promotion should intelligently, creatively, and persuasively communicate the benefits of cooperative education.

Promotion includes a whole set of communication alternatives. The two basic methods are public relations and advertising. Advertising includes any paid, non-personal presentation of the benefits of the cooperative education program by the community college, while public relations is provided free as a news service by the major media and is not "placed" in the sense that space or time is purchased by the college. For each promotional activity there is a distinctive media blend which the community college administrator must select. Before examining media alternatives, it is important that the administrative process for implementing promotion be considered.

Typically, a public relations or public information office, acting in a service staff capacity to each of the instructional arms of the college, provides the machinery for carrying out the promotion. However, the administrator responsible for the program frequently is involved in establishing objectives, planning, and laying out the message strategy for the promotion. That is, while the cooperative education administrator may not actually place the promotion or actively engage in certain production aspects of its preparation, he nonetheless is central to its conception and design in many institutions. In some smaller community colleges, the director of cooperative education or the appropriate division chairman may have complete authority for the promotion of the program. Additionally, the advisory committee structure for the community college can be invaluable in promoting the program, and its members should be encouraged to participate in the development of the promotion.

Regardless of the organizational arrangement for handling promotion, decisions about appropriate media are crucial to a thorough coverage of target clienteles (see especially Vickrey and Miller, 1973, pp. 12–14). The following media suggestions may be useful in promoting community college cooperative education programs.

Publicity and Advertising Media Suggestions

Brochures and Mailing Pieces. (1) A cooperative education brochure, which doubles as a direct mailing piece, presenting the benefits of the community college cooperative education program to students. (2) A cooperative education brochure, which could also double as a direct mailing piece, presenting the benefits of the community college cooperative education program to the employers. (Some colleges attempt to present both student and employer values in the same brochure, but if the budget permits, a more effective promotional strategy is to directly relate the cooperative education program to the needs of the target clientiele by preparing separate brochures.) The five-college consortium in California reports that approximately 50 percent of employers who responded to their promotional literature—brochures and letters—became active participants in the program. (3) A cooperative education newsletter that is mailed to all employers, students, and friends of the cooperative program informing them of latest program developments, the cooperative calendar, and important values of the program. (4) Letters on college letterheads directed to representative target clienteles for any of a series of promotional objectives (to introduce the program, to inform about some unusual program benefit, or perhaps to give attention to some outstanding employer or student).

Print and Electronic Communications. (1) Advertising placed in high school newspapers stressing the benefits of community college cooperative education. (2) Advertising placed in local trade and professional journals to stimulate employer interest in the program. (3) Advertising placed in local media (newspapers, TV, or radio) to describe benefits of the program (to the community, employers, or students, depending upon program requirements).

Sales Promotion Efforts. (1) Specialty advertising (key chains, pencils, calendars) to help remind the community of the existence of community college cooperative education. (2) Displays and exhibits of program successes set up for a variety of trade and industrial shows, county fairs, and shopping center programs. (3)

Presentation of the cooperative education program to high school classes, especially during career day programs. (4) Regular communication with high school guidance counselors and community personnel departments in order to inform them of the latest developments in the college's cooperative education program. (5) Special audio-visual presentations (slides and tapes or perhaps 16mm sound movies) of the program's operation and value to the community, employers, and students.

Public Relations. (1) Publicity of student and employer successes in local television, radio, and newspapers. (2) Publicity of unusual or noteworthy experiences of students in college media, such as the school newspaper. (3) Participation by students, employers, and the coordinator in interviews and group sessions with local media.

Unlimited promotional opportunities exist for the communication of cooperative education benefits to the community. The cooperative education administrator must be especially alert to these possibilities; he should put a total promotional program in writing, seeing that all target clienteles are reached. Miami-Dade Junior College's Roger Wadsworth gives this description of their promotional efforts (Lupton, Wadsworth, 1969, pp. 50–57):

> *A new program needs publicity and the Miami-Dade publicity department, student newspaper, duplicating services, and student activities center provided for publicity both internally (students and faculty) and outside (prospective cooperating employers) through news releases, posters, and brochures. With the audio visual department two slide-tape presentations were prepared oriented to the empolyer in one case and the student in the other. The program was listed with the Cooperative Education Association and in the College Bulletin. A newsletter was initiated modeled after that at South Florida, called the "Co-op," containing information for students, faculty, and employers of advances in the program as well as special calendar events and other significant material. Every opportunity to recruit community support for the new program was sought through*

speeches to business groups, personal contacts with business leaders, and special "Career Programs" in local high schools to reach potential student participants. A local television station provided outstanding publicity through its "Junior College Forum" series when the coordinator and several co-op students appeared on one of the telecasts.

C. J. Freund (1972, p. 31) emphasizes a special need for honesty in cooperative education promotion. He says that too often the "down-to-earth" or "product-oriented occupations" (traditional industrial jobs) are ignored by the popular media in favor of "high glamour" occupations (professional and social service jobs), and that colleges are frequently perpetuating the myth. He gives illustrations of this, and suggests that honest and straightforward communication about occupational realities is called for.

While Freund is concerned with promotion that does not clearly portray the business and commercial reality of work opportunities, P. E. Dubé complains that little attention is given to liberal arts cooperative education experiences: "Most descriptive literature is aimed primarily at students in specialized fields, e.g., the sciences, engineering, and business" (Dubé, 1971, p. 18). The problem is that students are portrayed in work positions which reflect their majors at the college (for example, data processing students operating computers, architectural drawing students drawing, nurses working in hospitals). Dubé suggests, "Promotional literature should be redesigned for the liberal arts student who is more likely to work on a co-op assignment that is related to his 'interests' rather than his 'major' " (1971, p. 18).

At a large comprehensive community college, promotion is typically initiated by departmental and divisional levels for a multiplicity of programs. A certain amount of puffery is likely because each program is prepared by the administrator responsible for it, but this should be guarded against by a system of checks and balances. Two positions taken in these pages impinge on the promotional effort: one, the advocacy of a commitment by the college to the kind of opportunities available to the student upon graduation; and two, a strategic as opposed to a tactical view of cooperative education in the community college as manifested in a comprehensive program.

Implementation of the first recommendation requires that the college be very careful in its statement of expected opportunities upon graduation from the college. In addition to keeping the college honest in its educational mission, all promotion should be as honest and fair as possible in portraying possible outcomes upon graduation. Obviously the college cannot and should not promise a particular result, but it can, on the other hand, establish recognition of its accountability for students upon graduation by outlining broad opportunities available to graduates. Some would argue that if colleges cannot fulfill their commitment to students then accreditation should be removed or the program dropped (Venn, 1967).

The second factor which impinges upon promotional efforts is the advocacy of a comprehensive cooperative program. The promotional implications of this are far-reaching, especially if the program is a mandatory one. The emphasis shifts from obtaining positive responses to a single program to communicating a whole new function and philosophy for the entire college. In a sense, promotion should create a new image of a "community" institution commited to and in partnership with the community in the achievement of its economic, social, and political objectives as well as its educational aims. The cooperative program should be presented as a revitalizing force in education. Promotion for the whole institution would then reflect the cooperative education aspect of its operation.

Nevertheless, the need would still exist for individual program promotions, and to the degree that coordination is decentralized, program bulletins should stress the cooperative education feature of their operation. General education and university parallel community college educators ought to stress the distinctive values of community college cooperative education, just as occupational educators have traditionally done in their promotional materials. Regardless of program area, the cooperative education message needs to be communicated clearly and persuasively in terms of its benefits to the community, the employer, and most important the student.

Defined Outcomes
in Cooperative
Education

★★★★★★★★★★★★★★★★★★★★★★★★★★★★★★★★★★★★★
★★★★★★★★★★★★★★★★★★★★★★★★★★★★★★★★★★★

A. M. Cohen in *Dateline '79* presents a hypothetical community college of the future. While there are many subtleties which differentiate this model from traditional community college education, there is one central change in conception, and that is the college's total commitment to defining outcomes for students. Learning is defined "as the changed capability for, or tendency toward, acting in particular ways" (1969, p. 57). Student performance is assessed before and after instruction. If no changes can be detected, inferences of learning cannot be made. Cohen writes, "The college spells out in advance—and accepts accountability for—the changes it expects to produce in its students, and often in its community. According to this concept, schools are media designed to cause changes in people and communities, and they are also uniquely qualified to define the direction of these changes." He clarifies, "In an institution using a defined-outcomes approach, goals are stated in such words as 'the student will learn to . . . ' rather than 'The college will provide . . . ' One approach depicts *ends,* the other *means;* one defines *product,* the other *process"* (1969, p. 161).

Defining Cooperative Education Outcomes

Robert Mager's *Preparing Instructional Objectives* establishes a formula for defining outcomes. He outlines three basic phases of the activity: "First, identify the terminal behavior by name; you can specify the kind of behavior that will be accepted as evidence that the learner has achieved the objective. Second, try to define the desired behavior further by describing the important conditions under which the behavior will be expected to occur. Third, specify the criteria of acceptable performance by describing how well the learner must perform to be considered acceptable" (1962, p. 12). It is not absolutely essential that each of these elements be present in an instructional objective, but the instructor-coordinator should work on the objectives so that they communicate the intended outcome of an educational experience. Defined outcomes should be written for all of the important terminal behaviors of a planned experience.

Clearly, the defined-outcomes approach can make an important contribution to instructional effectiveness. Because of the unusual circumstances associated with the cooperative education program—the college's absence of direct control over process, the heterogeneity of student work experiences, the diversity of individual student goals, and the employer's absence of familiarity with educational methodology—the use of the defined-outcomes approach is not clearly discernible. (See Fig. 9, p. 132.) The inability of some cooperative educators to specify the outcomes of a given experience has led some persons to see cooperative education as a kind of haphazard, imprecise, "shotgun" educational venture. Others would question whether cooperative education is education at all if it cannot specify terminal behavior.

In considering the nature of cooperative education, Wilson compares it with other forms of education (such as computer assisted education and higher education) : "What is common is that each, whether substantively, methodologically, or in terms of level, is a part of a process of behavioral change through experience. . . . Because the possibilities of change are almost infinite it is necessary that the particular behavior changes desired be specified" (1970, p. 2). Wilson considers cooperative education to be educationally valid because it is one important means, of a set of educational means, for providing conditions from which behavioral changes result. But how can behavioral changes be specified in cooperative education?

Wilson cites Tyler's perception of the educational activity as having three basic phases. The first phase is the specification of objectives or goals to be achieved by students, the second is the design of or identification of suitable learning experiences supportive of the goal, and the third is the evaluation of the extent to which the objectives are achieved (Wilson, 1972, p. 59). Wilson says of the "educative process" for cooperative education: "In collaboration with the individual student, goals are established that are responsive to the needs of the student. They may be goals which focus upon career development, upon personal development, or upon social development" (p. 60).

But a number of questions about the process involved must be dealt with. Should the employer, because of his important role in providing experiential learning, be involved in the objective-setting process? Should there be a distinction between student educational objectives and employer performance standards? And student's educational goals? And for goals which interrelate work and study? Should the student be involved in the setting of specific objectives for cooperative education work periods? How is the evaluation of the satisfactory completion of defined outcomes performed? Who should perform the evaluation: the student, the coordinator, or the employer? It is possible to conceive of at least four categories in which defined outcomes might be established. Consider the following basic categories of objectives (in order to simplify the presentation, they are labeled alphabetically).

Type (a) objectives are broad educational objectives that can be referred to as macro outcomes, in which the outcome of the entire program of cooperative education is set forth. These objectives suggest the kind of total product envisioned as a result of the completed program of integrated work and study, and they are clearly communicated to the student at the time of admission. For example, in the occupational realm: "The student shall be prepared to perform competently as a public accountant in the accounting office of a business enterprise or as an employee of an accounting firm, given the successful completion of two years of alternating work and study related to an accounting career as demonstrated by the performance of social, conceptual, and technical work skills critical to accounting occupations." In the university parallel program an illustrative type (a) objective might read: "The student shall transfer to the XYZ University as a first-quarter junior, given the successful completion of two years of alternating work and study experiences supportive of the student's educational aims and as demonstrated by the performance of social, conceptual, and technical skills critical to the student's choice of a discipline of study" (see Chapter Two). This class of objective is established by the college, and it is used as a guidance tool at the time of admission to help the student select a program on the basis of his own needs and educational ambitions.

Class (b) objectives are those established for the classroom dimension of the student's cooperative education experiences. These defined outcomes are of the class which Mager and Cohen allude to in their presentations of "instructional" objectives, and most references to behavioral objectives or defined outcomes in the literature imply this in-college instructional setting. This type of defined outcome will be categorized as a micro objective; it is supportive of the broader, more sweeping type (a) objective. An illustrative type (b) objective for a course in psychology might state: "The student will differentiate between the Freudian concepts of ego, id, and superego in a single paragraph during the completion of a written final examination in the last week of class with 90 percent accuracy." It is especially beneficial when a whole network of such objectives is established for each course in the curriculum. A desirable condition of these objectives would be that the student should be able to relate the principle, concept, or theory to his previous work experiences.

Class (c) objectives are particularly relevant to the activities of cooperative educators and can also be properly referred to as micro objectives. This class of objective establishes the defined outcomes for a particular work period. Performance standards for the work assignment are basic to this category of defined outcomes. Statement of type (c) objectives can be made by the cooperative education coordinator, but cooperative education's three-way involvement of student, employer, and college makes it desirable that each party be involved in the object-setting process. All three parties should if possible become participants in the objective-setting process.

Community colleges in the five-school cooperative education consortium in California have been experimenting with the use of the defined outcome approach. Their pioneering experiences provide much useful information for this discussion of type (c) objective development and implementation. Their plan for the design of type (c) objectives draws upon the inputs of coordinator, employer, and student. Arriving at a statement of defined outcomes for work periods with three persons involved may sound complicated and time consuming; in fact, it is a relatively simple process. Before reviewing such a plan, let us consider the rationale for the involvement of the three key persons in the cooperative education process.

In the managerial sciences an important behavioral principle advocated by many theorists is "management by objectives." This principle has had successful applications in industrial situations, in which a supervisor outlines the broad scope of the expectation for work performance to the managerial level he has responsibility for. The supervisor is careful not to program objectives as he sees them, instead he asks his managerial subordinates to establish objectives that will best satisfy department productivity and ultimately foster company success. This plan, sometimes referred to as a form of participative management, has experienced much success. The rationale is that employees who establish their own objectives typically will make a stronger commitment to accomplishing them, and in addition an improved *esprit de corps* is achieved as employees feel themselves to be more a part of the enterprise.

J. Fay offers the following arguments for the management-by-objectives approach in the cooperative education program: "The student should feel, this is my goal, set by me, for my advancement. . . . People are best motivated to work effectively toward an objective to which they are committed." He expands, "So, let us integrate the objectives by participation. Set the student's occupational objective so all three parties have an opportunity to profit by its achievement, and none can afford to loose sight of it" (1967, 1–2).

What is recommended for type (c) objectives is a merging of the defined-outcomes tactic for establishing instructional objectives, as advocated by Cohen, with the industrial model for management by objectives. The suggested merger also has implications for the formulation of type (b) as well as type (c) objectives. The setting of type (c) objectives ideally involves the participation of the employer, because only he can intelligently define the quantity and quality of performance a community college trainee can be expected to perform in the work position. Because cooperative education is a valid educational experience, and not just a form of part-time help for employers, the student's needs, educational aspirations, and abilities must certainly be an influence in the statement of objectives. The coordinator is vital to the process, because he possesses the necessary expertise to phrase meaningful defined outcomes in order to achieve a desired blending of employer and trainee emphasis. Similarly, evaluation should involve the participation of all three parties.

Vaughn Redding, Director of the Orange Coast and Golden West cooperative education programs, speaks glowingly of the success his college has experienced in the implementation of such a program. The following excerpts of steps students should follow in stating objectives, along with some sample objectives, are taken from the Orange Coast Community College "Cooperative Education Student Kit" (Redding, Garman, and Strandberg, 1971, pp. 5–6):

Steps for Establishing Objectives

    (1) The student should put in writing the objectives to be accomplished in terms of results.

    (2) The student should lay out a program for accomplishment of the objectives.

    (3) The student should secure understanding and approval of his superior. Objectives are most effective if they are discussed face-to-face between supervisor and student so that they may be mutually understood and accepted.

Some Considerations in Methodology for Preparing Objectives

The student should be encouraged to:

(1) *Avoid statements of objectives in generalities.*

(2) *Define an objective in terms of a single result.*

(3) *Be certain that he has the professional capability to specify the objective and the program for completion.*

(4) *Select language which can communicate to all interested parties, not to just a limited technical group.*

(5) *Identify his present position prior to solving problem objectives.*

(6) *Be certain that he knows what goals his organization is seeking so that his own objectives may coincide.*

Some Considerations for Instructor-Coordinators

Instructors may further the student's understanding and establishment of objectives by suggesting the following categories as a guide: (a) Routine duties, (b) Problem solving goals, (c) Creative goals, (d) Personal objective, and (e) Results-centered goals.

Examples of Objectives

A. *Routine Objectives*

(1) *To determine how to complete equipment checks each day by 3 P.M.*

(2) *To establish a routine for reporting all violations.*

B. *Problem Solving Objectives*

(1) *During this semester I will personally investigate all equipment failures to search for contributory causes of failure.*

(2) *During this semester I will collect data on and investigate all accident reports to determine a safety check list.*

C. *Creative Objectives*

(1) *By January to develop and introduce a statistical quality control system for the department.*

(2) *By June to develop an electronic order finding system in the warehouse.*

D. *Personal Objectives*

    (1) *During this semester to develop and improve presentation to customers.*

    (2) *During this semester to apply new methods in conference leading to those meetings I must lead.*

    (3) *During this semester to investigate and develop a format for improved report writing.*

    (4) *During this semester to be able to write a program for the computer.*

E. *Results—Centered Objectives*

    (1) *By February to revise a minimum of ten written and practical tests for industrial relations operations.*

    (2) *By February to have a practical knowledge of the use of a multi-meter.*

    (3) *By January to be able to recognize all schematic symbols pertinent to this company's equipment drawings.*

    (4) *By January to know how to set up and read the Tekstronix 545 oscilloscope for noise testing of potentiometers.*

    (5) *By January to be able to assemble wirewound and conductive plastic potentiometers.*

    (6) *During the semester I will install an accounting system for my department.*

At Orange Coast the coordinator meets with the student on campus during the first two weeks of the semester to discuss objectives for the cooperative work period. The student and employer meet after that to review possible objectives, and before the end of the ninth week the three parties meet to discuss the program, confirm objectives, and sign the agreement pledging their respective responsibilities. Before the sixteenth week of the semester the evaluation of the attainment of objectives is picked up by the coordinator. The job-oriented learning objectives form used by Orange Coast is reproduced in Exhibit D. Karl Strandberg did much pioneering of defined outcomes in cooperative education.

At the Cooperative Work Experience Education Workshop held at the Disneyland Hotel in February 1972, one of the special sessions headed by Karl Strandberg and Robert Barnett of Golden West and Compton Colleges in California revealed something of the reactions of employers to the plan: "The job-oriented learning objectives, according to one large employer, was the part of the program that turned them on. The idea that they could determine the learning experiences which would result in improved performance, improved safety, reduction in waste, and promotion opportunities was important to industry" (Barnett and Strandberg, 1972).

Sandra Hangley, a coordinator at Golden West College, reported on the successful use of class (c) defined outcomes as a group process at McDonnell Douglas and North American. Students "attended two group meetings this semester—in April an objective setting meeting, and in June an evaluation meeting. Even though meetings were on a group basis, the setting of objectives and evaluations were discussed individually with each student." At Xerox she reported that, "students were also handled as a group but in a somewhat different manner. The first meeting (setting of objectives) was held at the Xerox facility in Torrance. It was a group meeting which included both students and their supervisors. This approach provided a good opportunity for a three-way interaction between student, supervisor, and coordinator in the objective-setting process." She continued, "The second meeting (evaluation of objectives) was held on the Golden West Campus and included students and two supervisors" (Bennett and Redding, 1972, pp. 38–40).

Ms. Hangley commented on the instructional objectives approach to cooperative education: because the students lacked familiarity with the process of setting learning objectives for work experience, "a great deal more time was spent individually with each student. It was sometimes quite a struggle in the defining and the writing of these objectives. Yet it was a real learning experience, and a rather exciting one at that, for both the student and myself. . . . The evaluation meetings were primarily on an individual basis, with my meeting the student and employer separately. . . . In all instances the student and the employer had good communication prior to the meeting; therefore, the evaluation sessions were very open, constructive, and overall an extremely positive experience for both student and employer." She noted, "It might be mentioned at

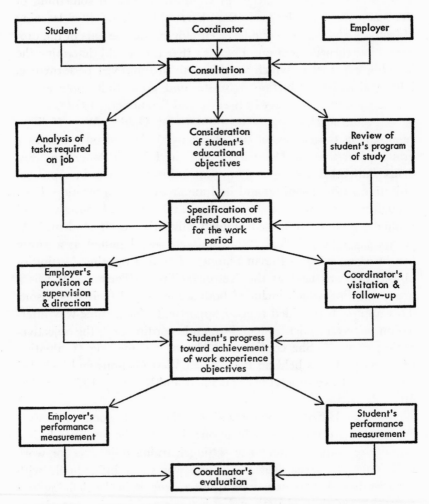

Figure 9. Tripartite Relationship in Defining and Evaluating
Cooperative Education Outcomes.

this time that a number of students verbalized positive feelings in the use of objectives, and felt this approach provided them the direction and incentive to do a better job. For the majority of miscellaneous employers this was their first experience with the job-oriented objective approach. All expressed satisfaction with it. A number of employers reported a distinct improvement in student attitudes on the job since using the objectives. Others were pleased to have specific criteria when evaluating the student as opposed to a 'vague progress form' " (Bennett and Redding, 1972, p. 42).

The participation of employer, student, and coordinator is a realistic and attainable system for specifying type (c) defined outcomes. The advantages of planning such an arrangement far outweigh the disadvantages of an occasional administrative headache. It offers the special advantages of using the defined-outcome methology to specify learner behavior, which involves the participation of the cooperative education tripartite in a management-by-objectives scheme, and of intensifying the educational value of the cooperative education work experience period. It eliminates the traditional checklist (evaluation form) used by many college cooperative education staffs, on which the employer rates a student (excellent, average, poor, etc.) on a set of factors, such as human relations, work skills, punctuality, and grooming. The learning objectives approach permits a truly individualized program that specifically addresses itself to critical work tasks and trainee needs.

Type (d) objectives are also of the micro category and are equally significant to the achievement of type (a) macro objectives. This class of defined outcome focuses on the kindling of two types of interrelationships; the first is the interplay of classroom theory with particular work experiences, and the second is the interface between the total cooperative education program and the educational goals of the student. To this end, type (d) objectives can be advantageously attained via a student report required in conjunction with a related cooperative education class or practicum, as La Guardia Community College refers to it, or simply the requirement of a report without a related classroom session.

Sinclair Community College in Ohio has implemented a report structured around defined outcomes as a part of a contract grading system in certain of its cooperative occupational programs.

The report is designed to cause students to interrelate study and work experiences. Each successive letter grade provides for consideration of an additional work-study relationship, and the statement of requirements for each grade level is set forth in a defined outcomes format. Each successive grade letter, from C to B and B to A, indicates increased thoroughness, quantitatively and qualitatively, in the development of the report. Exhibit B reproduces a portion of the contract grade plan for students enrolling in this program.

Type (d) objectives should cause the student to consider his work experience in terms of his classroom instruction and his personal, educational, or occupational goals. For example, assuming enrollment as an occupational major, the student should be asked periodically to reevaluate his career objectives in lieu of his most recent work period; has he confirmed his career choice or is he less clear about his "fit" to the work in that field? In addition, the report should require the student to relate his general and technical education courses to his cooperative work experience period. The Borough of Manhattan Community College utilizes an interesting report format in its occupational program (see Exhibit B). Type (d) objectives verified through a written report or similar medium should not be limited to occupational programs alone; exploration, transfer, and general education students can also benefit from an approach that requires them to relate their work experience to their program and their personal and educational pursuits.

An evaluation of the student during his classroom period is facilitated by examining how well he has accomplished type (b) objectives. Similarly, the assignment of a grade in the student's work experience period, whether it be the traditional letter grade or some form of pass-fail, should consider inputs from student, employer, and coordinator with regard to the attainment of *both* class (c) and (d) objectives. Both objectives need to be measured before inferences of learning can be made.

An example will clarify the need for evaluating both type (c) and type (d) objectives. An employer might "dock" a student for shoddy work practices and a lack of enthusiasm during the work period, but an examination of the written report, structured around type (d) objectives, might show that the student had changed career objectives because of a significant event during the work period that led him to become disillusioned with his work. That learning experience might be extremely valuable for the student and might justify, in the coordinator's opinion, something other than a failing grade for the work experience period. Similarly, a program that uses only work reports without type (c) objective specification and evaluation could tend to force down the grades of students who have difficulty communicating verbally, even though their employers may have evaluated their work performance as quite satisfactory. Visits with the student and employer at work are indeed desirable, but they simply cannot take the place of a careful evaluation of both the (c) and (d) objectives.

Some Additional Thoughts on Preparing Objectives

The preparation of type (b), (c), and (d) objectives for occupational students and type (c) objectives for all other students should proceed from a consideration of the nature of the work to be performed (Mager and Beach, 1967, pp. 1–6). A thorough consideration of all aspects of the work should be prerequisite to a statement of defined outcomes for a unit of instruction or work experience period, and when the objective is stated it should be directly supportive of the attainment of those critical work skills. The instructor-coordinator's previous work experiences and educational training in his occupational specialty will be of value in this process, but it should not be depended upon entirely. Feedback from the cooperative employer, the advisory committee, cooperative students, and community surveys are certainly significant sources of information from which to develop learning objectives. Increasingly, research specialists in each of the occupational specialties have taken on the responsibility of specifying critical tasks for occupational categories based upon samplings of managers, technicians, and others engaged in the activity. For example, in the area of marketing and retailing, Lucy Crawford has completed a study of work tasks and their associated competencies for a series of distributive occupations (1969), Harland E. Samson has recently published a careful study of the responsibilities of middle management retail personnel (1969), and Carmichael has completed a similar study to detect

Table 4
Four Types of Defined Outcomes

Category of Objectives	Type (a)	Type (b)	Type (c)	Type (d)
Central Characteristic	Broad program objectives	Classroom objectives	Work period objectives	Interface of study and work objectives
Scope	Macro	Micro	Micro	Micro
Objective Setter	Program director in conjunction with advisory committee	Classroom instructor along with student inputs	Coordinator, employer, and student	Instructor-coordinator along with student inputs
Nature of Outcome	Defines outcomes of completion of entire work-study program	Defines outcomes upon completion of unit of study	Defines the outcomes of completion of cooperative work period	Defines outcomes of interrelating work and study and their impact on achieving educational objectives
Experiences Necessary for Achievement	Completion of associate degree requirement	Learning activities provided in class, and preferably related to work experience	Work experiences achieved via the cooperative work period	Consideration of the relationship of work and study periods via a written report

critical managerial activities of middle management in retailing (1970)'.

Warren Meyer stresses the need for a careful consideration of the differences in occupational competency patterns within occupational fields before the construction of objectives. He suggests that the critical factors in formulating defined outcomes are the needs of the students to be served, the requirements of the occupation for which training is pursued, and the role of an idealized citizen worker. Factors which influence the expected student outcomes, and which should be considered in a statement of defined outcomes, include characteristics of the students to be served, educational achievement level of the program, and characteristics of the local community and school (Meyer 1969, pp. 24–26).

In summary, it is important that community college cooperative educators be familiar with the management-by-objectives and defined-outcomes approaches to setting objectives in four distinct areas. Table 4 lists the characteristics of each objective type.

Classroom Perspectives

Charles F. Kettering, one of this country's renowned engineers, strongly supported cooperative education and its application in higher education (Wilson, in Knowles, *Handbook of Cooperative Education,* 1971, p. 13). By the use of a metaphor he clarified the advantages of a cooperative education versus traditional education; he compared the conventional process of intensive classroom study joined at its completion by an abrupt shift to full-time employment to the conventional butt-welding process and the cooperative method of work and study integration with the technologically superior lap-welding process. (The superiority of lap welding is due to the overlapping of adjoining parts, which makes for a greatly strengthened bond in contrast to the butt weld process, which is merely the welding of the edge of one piece with the edge of another.) The alternation of work and study provides a significantly superior education, but the "lap welding" process can be further strengthened by activities that reinforce classroom work. The remainder of this chapter will consider non-work learning designed to optimize cooperative education. Specifically, the following will be explored:

classroom instruction, cooperative student reports, and the granting of degree credit.

As suggested earlier, a cross fertilization of work and study experiences is largely up to the faculty member. Ideally, instructors ought to encourage students to critically examine theories and principles presented in class during their work periods and, upon their return to the classroom, faculty members should draw upon individual student experiences, structure group discussion based on learning that took place on the job, and assign reports that require students to reevaluate the work period in relation to important concepts advocated in class. (In doing these things, the instructor is acting as an "experiential integrator".) This process of relating work to classroom study should not be thought of as a function appropriate only for occupational educators; to the degree that a comprehensive cooperative education program is offered, all faculty members should be encouraged, perhaps through special in-service training sessions conducted by cooperative education personnel, to stimulate students to relate work and study experiences. A faculty committed to this learning procedure can achieve new depths of understanding, greatly strengthening the educational impact of cooperative education.

In addition to the arranging of regular classroom activities to the work experience of students, special related classes can be offered to prepare the student for his work assignment and to reinforce work-period learning experiences. Two variations of a cooperative education class are desirable. The first course shall be referred to as the "career orientation" class; it has as its major objective the preparation of students for their work assignments. The second class shall be referred to as a "career practicum," and is offered in a sequence of sections concurrently with the student's enrollment for work experience. The scheduling pattern, contact hour arrangement, and credit hour equivalent varies markedly from community college to community college. It is recommended that the career orientation course be offered during the term immediately prior to the student's first work experience period; it should meet a minimum of two contact hours a week, and should be allocated a minimum of one to three credit hours, depending on course requirements; and it should be a prerequisite to enrollment in the first work experience period and should be taught by instructor-coordinators. The career practicum course should be a concurrent requirement for enrollment in a work experience period, should meet a minimum of one contact hour a week, and unlike the career orientation class should be scheduled so that all students with like or similar majors can be grouped together. Excellent instructional materials by Bennett (1973) and Chapman (1973) might be considered for adoption in either "career orientation" or "practicum" classes.

The purpose of the career orientation course is to develop work related attitudes to facilitate smooth articulation to the work assignment. This class should be designed to provide a general orientation, not to give instruction in specific work skills, and it should be open, in a comprehensive program, to students of varying interests, majors, and career orientations. Human relations skills in work settings, interviewing procedure, data sheet preparation, communication principles, pre-employment testing, Social Security and related work laws, and procedural aspects of the cooperative education program are central to the career orientation class.

The Borough of Manhattan Community College conducts a class of this type for two contact hours a week for two units of credit. Manhattan uses case studies, role playing, written assignments, and informal meetings with industrial and government leaders. Among the activities in this class are the preparation of a paper by the student which analyzes his strengths and weaknesses, the administration and interpretation of interest tests, the examination of case studies involving human relations, management, and communications topics, an examination of the history and philosophy of cooperative education, a review of materials on job titles and occupational information, a look at occupational trends and employment needs, a review of procedures for writing a resumé and interviewing, and the making of selected field trips to business or government agencies. Requirements for the Manhattan career preparation class include short papers, a book review, a term project, and a mid-term and final exam. The class is taught by cooperative education coordinators.

The career orientation class is a one-term class and permits students from a broad cross section of studies to meet and talk together about their fears, preoccupations, and observations about entering a new work endeavor. A seminar atmosphere is desirable, within the constraints of a controlled but informal structure. Learning objectives should be assigned for the whole class and specific defined outcomes, preferably individualized ones tailored to meet varying student interests, should be established. The course should orient students to the philosophy and procedure of the cooperative education program, encourage self-analysis to ascertain personal strengths and weaknesses, set forth the procedure for job application, present the case for good managerial and human relations abilities, provide information on broad occupational changes and shifts in the economy, and clarify the responsibilities of the student to the college and employer.

Miami-Dade Junior College conducts a class similar in concept to the career orientation class recommended here. An unusual aspect of this class is that it is open to both cooperative and non-cooperative students who are exploring careers; the course is called "career orientation workshop." Miami-Dade gives this description of the course: "This workshop is open to all students who want to know more about businesses in the Miami area from guest speakers, need aid in obtaining a job, or aid in the selection of a proper career. . . . Requirements include taking vocational and personality inventories, being counseled, and listening to five speakers (Miami-Dade, 1971)". Broward Community College in Fort Lauderdale, Florida, requires a similar one-semester-hour course called "cooperative education seminar," which is designed to acquaint the student with procedural aspects of the program.

The career practicum class is designed to reinforce classroom and work experiences. The class can be instrumental in securing Kettering's notion of lap welding by emphasizing the cooperative education experience. It is desirably taught by the student's coordinator using outside resource speakers; this arrangement is especially effective if coordination is decentralized and faculty are responsible for the work experience aspect of the program. Students with similar program majors or career objectives should attend the same career practicum. At La Guardia Community College, students select a practicum based upon a variety of alternative themes related to his own objectives.

He might choose from among such practicum themes as these:

"today's secretary," "the psychology of work," "retailing: a new look," "banking: an innovative service industry," "the social role of business," and "dynamics of the learning environment." The concurrent practicum arrangement advocated here works best with an alternating block system, but numerous variations on this theme are possible in a variety of alternations. A written report and seminar discussion are basic to this course, in which class activities are directed toward bridging the gap between work and study. Role playing, case studies, group discussions, and career games find application in these settings.

The opportunity of discussing with other students those problems and experiences occurring during a particular work period is an important bonus of the practicum. The class also provides an opportunity for the student to confer with the coordinator about his work experience and its relationship to his objectives and program of study. The student also finds that the problems he has experienced are often not unique, but are shared by other students in similar situations.

An interesting variation on the practicum, the concurrent work experience class, is practiced by the College of the Mainland in Texas, where it is called their "24 hour a day learning experience." Each cooperative education period has its own separate course number and associated learning activities. A syllabus of roughly thirty pages and requirements for the period are provided to the student. The reading and reviewing of at least eight technical articles related to the job, a written job description, and other requirements are a part of this "package" for the first quarter. Later quarters require the student to critically evaluate his employer's organization and to apply managerial principles to his work. In addition to these job-related assignments, students complete a second phase which includes general education activities. Examples of this include the implementation of a particular social activity, the study of human relations in an individualized course, and in latter terms, the interviewing of community officials, the presentation of the College to a community group, the observation of a current issue and a written expression of the student's views (to be sent to his Congressman), and the consideration of personal management factors such as personal finance, credit, and insurance (Lupton and McNutt, 1972, pp. 62–63).

The major thrust of this course and the written reports required in it is to help students interrelate classroom and work experiences and to help them recognize the important values to be gained from the cooperative education learning experience. These broad objectives apply for the complete sequence of practicums, although the subject matter and specific objectives for each practicum will vary. A defined-outcomes approach can be used with great success, and the specification of outcomes is especially useful for individual assignments within the practicum—particularly the written report.

Many colleges require a written report by the student during the cooperative period. In addition to Sinclair Community College and College of the Mainland, Manhattan, Broward, Northwood, Merritt, Miami-Dade, Pasadena City, and Compton two-year colleges require some variation of a work report from their cooperative students. At Merritt College, students enrolled for credit in the cooperative program write a report that "increases in the degree of self-analysis and job relatedness as the student progresses in the program." At Northwood Institute's "externship" program, a written report accounts for 50 percent of the final grade with the other 50 percent based on the employer's evaluation. The report includes a history of the company, a job description, and an analysis of the relationship of classroom theory to the work setting. Broward Community College and Compton College also require a report, and the student's grade for the work experience is a combination of employer evaluation and thoroughness of the report. At Miami-Dade, cooperative students may select independent study projects in conjunction with their work experience; reports focus on the responsibility and environment of the work assignment or written summaries of the book *The Student in Society* (Lupton, 1969). Excerpts from student reports written at a midwestern community college (Sinclair Community College in Dayton, Ohio) suggest the breadth of candid and self-critical student responses that such a report may elicit:

"I have been able to develop an ability to work directly with customers. . . . A weakness that I have discovered is

a failure on my part to see all sides of a situation and the people involved when changes within the organization have been made."

"Perhaps the best thing I have accomplished thus far is learning how to get along with the people I work with in the office. . . . As far as weak points are concerned, I know that I must improve my accounting skills such as journal entries, posting, footing, etc. . . . I am looking forward to the Auditing and Federal Tax courses I will take next quarter."

"I have found that while working at XYZ Company I have learned how to make better use of my time. I've learned how to structure my time. . . . My weakest point is the fact that I am forgetful."

Students may comment on academic experiences and changes in educational objectives related to their jobs:

"Chemistry was really valuable for me when I was called upon by the company to work in the Processing Division. . . . Statistics helped me considerably with my work in the Technical Data Control Section of the Manufacturing Standards Department."

"Cost accounting was by far the most important course. . . . Since I am responsible for keeping the costs in the service department, both school and work have run hand in hand . . . work and school really tied together this quarter. My schooling made my job easier, and my job made my schooling easier."

"Time spent on the computer has been valuable to my work, but in my opinion the amount of time provided for student use isn't enough. Many times the system is closed when students need to run programs . . . [the system] often gets interrupted for administrative work on teacher's jobs which should be set up for some other time."

"When I first enrolled at the College I had plans of taking the required courses for the Retailing degree as quickly as possible so that I would have the qualifications for becoming a fashion buyer. . . . However, since my employment at PDQ Department Store my objectives have changed considerably. I soon learned I was too conservative to stay abreast of the fashion world. . . . I also found that there was more paperwork and details to buying than I had ever imagined."

Co-op students are frequently asked to appraise their program in the work experience report:

"I feel that my experience this quarter has helped me, especially in my personal development and career preparation. . . . Although I am not able to continue in the co-op program I sincerely feel it has been one of the most rewarding parts of my education up to this point. . . . and truly one of the finest aspects of the curriculum here."

"My co-op work experience has been most valuable, especially because of my financial situation. Due to my wife's pregnancy, this job has enabled me to meet my expenses and pay the College's tuition fees."

Students may bring up any of a number of sensitive work problems —including handling a love interest:

"Besides new learning this quarter at work, I started seeing one of the girls who also worked in this department, and this was the first time I had ever gone with someone I worked with. . . . At the beginning it was really rough because I wanted to talk to her all the time. It took me awhile to realize that my social life wasn't acceptable during working hours."

Specifically, the cooperative education reports, whether required in a career practicum course or handled independently of a class, should deal with the following kinds of issues and problems:

(1) The influence of the work experience on student career

goals (if a career student) or on the perception of future career plans (if a general education student).

(2) Student observations concerning changed perceptions of personal strengths and weaknesses.

(3) The relationship to the work situation of specific principles or concepts studied in class.

(4) The kinds of cognitive, attitudinal, or psychomotor skills learned on the job which related to the student's course of study.

(5) Analysis of major work adjustments made during the work period and an indication of the success experienced in overcoming the problems that led to them.

(6) The importance of interpersonal relationships in achieving the institution's objectives and the student's own personal fulfillment.

(7) The significance of general education courses (such as sociology, communications, and literature) for the work situation.

(8) Critical incidents, successful or unsuccessful, that the student observed on the job.

Practice reveals that most community colleges do not use a formal class arrangement (a practicum) but use the cooperative report in lieu of a class. Reports vary widely in their requirements; some require two to three pages, others require ten to fifteen pages, most require that the report be typed, and nearly always a deadline is established for the report. Dawson suggests (1972, p. 8), "The major purpose of the cooperative work report, required of the students, is to stimulate the student's observations and learning during the job period. As such it provides the rationale for allocating college credit for cooperative work (along with the employer's evaluation of the student's job performance)."

Granting Cooperative Education Credit

It would seem perfectly obvious that cooperative education should be granted academic credit. However, there is not unanimity on this position. Those educators opposed to the granting of credit sometimes use these arguments: (1) cooperative education cannot be rigidly controlled as in a classroom environment; (2) students during work terms may not be required to use intellectual rigor; (3)

if credit is granted for co-op, the same logic can be used in granting credit for any life experience; (4) universities which accept our transfers will not look favorably upon co-op credit; (5) accrediting bodies may not be approving of credit for co-op (see Wilson, 1973, pp. 33–34). The previous discussion in this chapter is extremely critical to this question. *The defined outcome methodology, or a system like it, which focuses on specific learning goals of students, arranges experiences supportive of those objectives, and provides evaluation to determine the extent of learning is essential to the verification of educational validity of cooperative education (and its credit worthiness).* While control over learning variables, credit transferability, and perceptions of accrediting agencies require administrative attention, the primary thrust of cooperative education's contribution is demonstrable behavioral change in students—significant learning which mandates the granting of credit. Wilson's study of cooperative education collegiate programs indicates that 69 percent of two-year colleges grant non-additive (applying toward the student's degree) credit for work experience; in about 63 percent of the two-year colleges, three to four hours of credit is granted per term of work experience, and 77 percent of the colleges grant credit through the cooperative department (1972, p. 13). It is this "non-additive" feature which is of most concern to students, because it means little to a student to receive credit when it does not in fact apply toward his two-year degree. David R. Opperman states, "If it is to be meaningful, academic credit for co-op experiences must not be "add-on" credit. This is only a bookkeeping scheme which defeats the objective of allowing the student to use the education he acquired off-campus in partial fulfillment of his degree requirements" (1972, p. 802).

While the figures are not conclusive, there is a strong movement toward granting degree credit for the work experience aspect of cooperative education programs. Given the previous plan for related cooperative education classes or work reports, it is recommended that the career placement course be granted one to three credit hours and the concurrent career practicum be granted credit as part of a work experience "package." This package of work experience and weekly attendance in a practicum might be designated from two to six credit hours, depending upon state requirements and the calendar of the college (quarter, semester, or trimester).

In discussing the case for academic credit in cooperative education, Opperman cites a meeting of university and college presidents at the University of South Florida in February 1970, at which the granting of academic credit for co-op work experiences was examined. The presidents in general felt that if the work experience was relevant it should be granted credit, and one president suggested that the time had come for college administrations to realize that learning comes from the community as well as the classroom (1971, p. 800). J. Dudley Dawson maintains (1972), "If a college values the educational worth of cooperative work experience, to the extent of recommending or requiring it as an integral part of its program, then it would seem only reasonable to allow a limited amount of degree credit for it."

New impetus for the granting of credit for cooperative education work experience came about in 1968, when the Cooperative Education Division of the ASEE recommended that credit be granted for cooperative education work experience, and in 1971, when the Joint Cooperative Education Association and the ASEE Cooperative Education Division Academic Credit Committee presented a report to the two groups calling for the granting of credit for off-campus experiences. This recommendation was based on a survey of 96 colleges, over 2000 students, and 39 large employers of students (Opperman, 1971, p. 802).

Opperman offers this mandate to cooperative education colleges for the granting of academic credit: "Colleges and universities have often been accused of reacting instead of acting. Here is a real opportunity for the academic institutions to show their sincerity in making their programs more relevant by acting positively now to grant academic credit for off-campus co-op experiences instead of waiting for some future crisis" (1971, p. 802).

From the student's point of view, cooperative education is infinitely more palatable if it recognizes occupational experience as counting toward graduation requirements. It legitimizes the program, but more important it "puts teeth" in the claim that cooperative education is educationally relevant.

★★★★★★★★★★★★★ 9 ★★★★★★★★★★★★★
★★★★★★★★★★★★★ ★★★★★★★★★★★★★

The Student
and
Experiential Learning

★★★★★★★★★★★★★★★★★★★★★★★★★★★★★★★★★★
★★★★★★★★★★★★★★★★★★★★★★★★★★★★★★★★★★

An educational system includes more than context, process, product, and feedback subsystems. There must be an input activity to provide a smooth articulation from the student's previous environment to that of college and work. A thoughtful introduction to the diversity of program offerings and a careful assessment of the student's capabilities, orientations, and objectives is crucial to his selection of learning experiences that will satisfy his needs. Because of the impact that a comprehensive cooperative education activity (mandatory or optional) has when programmed with the ongoing community college function, it is inconsistent with the philosophy of a fully integrated program to distinguish between a work input process and a study input process. Students may well believe that classroom study is important in the attainment of learning objectives (as discussed in Chapter Eight) but that cooperative work experience is another kind of endeavor and not supportive of those same objectives.

The Critical Guidance Function

The input system to be sketched in this chapter has two dimensions: the testing or assessment of student needs, and the presentation of program options. The student services staff has the reponsibility for this, in conjunction with the cooperative education department (at the time of admission), and the process is aided by the use of a cooperative education student handbook. The cooperative education department must necessarily have an extremely close working relationship with guidance personnel, keeping them constantly informed of their activities, while in return the guidance staff supplies necessary feedback to cooperative personnel. The student services staff has responsibility for administering the battery of tests for new students. Advising the student requires a full knowledge of his personal and career orientations, and it is therefore desirable that college testing be thorough and comprehensive. Tests of intelligence, educational achievement, and aptitude, as well as personality measurements and preference tests (interests), are all desirable.

Data generated from these tests can be exceedingly useful in conjunction with a personal interview in which the student discusses his prior experiences and his attitudes toward work and life. The objective of this phase of the interview is to help the student consider his aptitudes, personality, present frame of reference, knowledge of self, and interests, in order to determine his needs. Typical community college student need-clusters, derived from the taxonomy presented in the model in Chapter Two, are outlined to the student to help him decide about his personal orientation and most appropriate program of study.

The special benefits of combining work and study experiences are presented to the student. This is a particularly important aspect of the interview because the college, while not guaranteeing a specific result upon graduation, does suggest the nature of the options available upon completion of the degree. The student's anxiety will diminish when he sees the opportunities available to him upon successful completion of the two-year degree. This approach provides the additional bonus of instilling a sense of purpose in the student, a desire to perform well in the program in order to achieve these objectives. The student services personnel do not overburden the student with detailed course information and various program requirements; rather, they refer him to an instructor-coordinator, arranging a specific appointment, providing copies of the college bulletin and (more important) the cooperative education handbook for him to read prior to the meeting. (In this discussion, we assume decentralized coordination conducted by faculty members; see Chapters Two and Five for details.)

The student meets with his instructor-coordinator after his initial contacts with guidance personnel. The instructor-coordinator acts as his advisor, cooperative coordinator, and periodic instructor in selected courses for as long as the student's needs (and declaration of program major) remain the same. A special effort should be made to stress to the student that he need not feel committed to a particular program area (or coopportunity cluster, as suggested in the model) and that he can change his plan of study very easily as he makes new discoveries about his own needs. The first interview with the designated instructor-coordinator is a very useful meeting. The student is given more detail about his program of study. The specific values of cooperative education are explained, and the student's responsibilities in the program are reviewed. The Cooperative Education Handbook is reviewed and the student information form is administered. Seaverns (1970, p. 24) suggests the following purposes of this interview: "(1) to establish rapport; (2) to obtain information; (3) to give information; (4) to motivate students (the interview provides the coordinator with an excellent opportunity to stimulate the *thinking, feeling,* and *action* on the part of the student)."

Seaverns calls this first interview with the coordinator the "preliminary" or "screening" interview, at which time all important facts about the student are gathered. The second meeting, the "selection" interview, takes place during an early study period, at which time the student and coordinator explore training opportunities that may offer experiences related to the student's goals. The meeting usually takes place during the quarter in which the student's "career orientation" class is discussing interview techniques, appropriate work habits, personal appearance, and resumés. The third meeting, the "placement" interview, is used to provide specifics about the work placement, including instructions about the job description and specification, salary, hours, fringe benefits, probable rotation plan, and of particular importance, instructions for the student's interview with the company and an explanation of the use of the student introduction card. Upon securing employment for the student, the coordinator, student, and employer arrange a meeting at the beginning of the work period, at which time the defined outcomes are established for the term. Later, the "progress and adjustment" interview allows for a discussion of the student's performance on the job, as revealed by the employer's evaluation of defined outcomes and the student's work report. In addition, the coordinator attempts to discover whether the student wants to remain at the same work site during the next work period. These interviews should be planned in light of the student's schedule (the coordinator is supplied with a copy of this schedule) and the responsibilities of the coordinator. Postcards sent to the student, the posting of an interview schedule, or telephone notification can be used to communicate the interview date, time, and place (Seaverns, 1970, p. 24; also see Miller in Knowles' *Handbook of Cooperative Education,* 1971, p. 157).

Merritt College in Oakland, California, operates a cooperative education program with an integral guidance and counseling component. Carolyn Schuetz, director of the program, comments: "There is a strong counseling element to our program. Students enrolled have access to academic, vocational, and personal counseling specially geared to their needs as employed students" (Schuetz, 1972). Similarly, La Guardia Community College's cooperative education department stresses counseling done in close cooperation with student services personnel. Its students meet regularly in small groups during study periods in what is called "advisory hours" with a counseling staff member, a teaching faculty member, and a cooperative advisor. They refer to the pre-work experience interval as the "preparation period." Specifically, they try to help the student in the following ways: "(1) assess his own experience, strengths and weaknesses; (2) build the confidence to project his strengths, especially in an interview; (3) begin to develop career goals; (4) identify goals for internship; (5) identify skills necessary for a particular internship or career; (6) understand the employer's goals and needs, and what he will expect of the intern; (7) understand the philosophy and procedures of the La Guardia program and his responsibilities to it; (8) select initial internship in context of larger goals" (La Guardia Community College communiqué, 1972).

The interview phase with the guidance staff and the instructor-coordinator is critical to successfully introducing new students into the program. However, a second phase of this activity deserves attention, and that is the development and dissemination of a cooperative education student handbook. Information in the handbook should be presented in a concise, creative, and interesting manner. Important matters which deserve treatment in the handbook include the following (grouped arbitrarily into four paragraphs):

1. An introduction to cooperative education at the community college. Values of cooperative education to the student. Typical experiences of cooperative students at the community college. Presentation of broad patterns of student needs. Outline of program offerings designed to service these needs (specification of broad outcomes of graduation from the program). A flow chart specifying the kinds of work and educational options the student has open to him given his program selection (see Chapter Two for illustration). Brief consideration of the requirements of each of the program clusters (without detailing course requirements and credit hour equivalents).

2. Overview of cooperative education program operation. Calendar for the year. Interview schedule with instructor-coordinator. Role of the instructor-coordinator. Referral and placement procedure. Role of the employer. Student responsibilities in the program. Visitation procedure.

3. Educational factors. Defining outcomes during the work period (presentation of form, sample objectives, and rationale). Evaluation of performance on the job. The cooperative education career orientation class. The cooperative education practicum class. Written report requirements. Cooperative work experience grade procedure, if any.

4. Details of program operation. Forms: (a) Work attendance record: specific hours worked signed by supervisor, and to be returned to coordinator at the end of the quarter along with a (b) current schedule: student indicates work hours and classes he is taking that quarter, if any. Procedure for scheduling: Work and study periods. Vacations and holidays. Conditions of employment. Changing jobs or resignation. Absence from work. Social Security information. Selective Service deferment.

The College of San Mateo and Orange Coast Community Colleges in California and Broward Community College in Florida have prepared excellent cooperative education handbooks or manuals for their students. These fine examples could be used as models in preparing handbooks for other community colleges. Nevertheless, there is some danger that the student handbook will seem to remove the need for close and direct communication about the program between coordinators and students (E. R. Billings, 1971). What is clearly needed is a *combination* of personal counseling and an effectively written handbook.

Serving Disadvantaged Students

The potential of community college cooperative education for providing a significantly more meaningful education for disadvantaged students is just being recognized. Because many community colleges have an open-door admissions policy, a guidance emphasis, developmental education, and an urban location near pockets of poor in the inner city, they are in a position to make an important contribution in this regard. Additionally, cooperative education modified community colleges offer new hope for disadvantaged students in the form of financial aid accruing from work experience periods, pertinent social and occupational experiences which augment studies, and accelerated assimilation in the economic, political, and social structures of the community.

While cooperative education is first and foremost an educational program, for certain minorities and students from socioeconomically deprived backgrounds, the chance to earn money is a prime attraction. This financial implication is important because it allows some students to defray the costs of a college education.

Dawson states, "Many disadvantaged students cannot even enter a publicly supported college, much as they may desire it, without financial assistance. Since in many cases the family assistance is non-existent, the financial need goes beyond the cost of college fees, books, transportation, and incidentals to include clothes, medical services, and other personal expenses" (1971, p. 13).

A federally funded program designed to stimulate financial assistance for disadvantaged college students by providing employment was made possible by amendments to the Higher Education Act. This legislation provided for the College Work-Study Program, which is implemented in community college programs as well as in four-year colleges and universities. The Work-Study Program is often confused with cooperative education, but not only are the two usually administered differently but at present they have distinctly different aims, being similar only in that they place students in jobs. The primary aim of the Work-Study Program is to provide financial aid for disadvantaged students by employment in non-profit institutions, and it is typically administered through the college's business office or financial aid department (Lupton, 1970, and Klein et al., 1968).

Former President Lyndon Johnson stated, "More than one hundred thousand young people too poor to afford college have found, through the college work-study program, an opportunity for higher education—and a chance to fulfill their dreams. Through them, we are keeping faith with the highest ideals of our past, and a covenant with the future" (Farrell, 1965, p. 2). Students in this program are from families with low incomes, incomes frequently less than $3000 a year. They attend classes full-time at the college and work part-time in jobs in public institutions. The program is designed to allow them to see prospects for themselves beyond the unskilled jobs that they identify with their families, as well as to generate income to defray expenses.

Basically, two categories of placements were recognized in this legislation: one, professionally oriented positions with non-profit, service agencies that have some relationship to the student's career objectives; or, two, positions on campus. Unfortunately, the campus positions have been the primary recipients of government monies, and the social services have been slighted. James E. Allen,

Jr., U. S. Commissioner of Education, said at the Atlanta Service-Learning Conference on June 30, 1969: "Of the 350,000 young people taking part in the College Work-Study Program, most have been employed in their campuses. We would like to see the ratio reversed, with the majority off-campus" (Lupton, 1970, p. 34). D. Keith Lupton has observed, "Too many students are running errands, duplicating, filing, cutting pieces of paper into smaller pieces, and similar activities. Fortunately, the law did prohibit maintenance type work" (1970, p. 40).

Lupton argues for bringing the Work-Study Program under the administration of the cooperative education staff, for increasing the educational relevance of the program by placing students in meaningful work in non-profit agencies related to their career objectives (successfully done by Pasadena College), and for stimulating liberal arts cooperative education by adapting Work-Study provisions to the special needs of non-business and engineering students (1970, p. 40). Through the Federal Work-Study Program and cooperative education needy students will obtain financial rewards critical to their continued enrollment at the college. But the important distinction is that financial gain is only one aspect of the cooperative education service to the disadvantaged student.

One major thrust of cooperative education is to provide work and study of personal relevance to the student and the potential for an improved self-concept; these values are translated into a higher retention of students. Dawson notes (1971, p. 14): "The educationally unprepared student, who rarely has a history of academic achievement, will usually do better on a cooperative job than he will do on his studies. . . . Maslow has cited the fact that important changes occur within the individual who identifies himself with meaningful work, and that this identification is a way of overcoming human shortcomings." (The relationship of cooperative education to the achievement of needs, using Maslow's hierarchy, is explored by Patricia M. Rowe in the *Journal of Cooperative Education* article "Motivation and Job Satisfaction on the Work Term of Cooperative Students," November 1970.)

An additional benefit of personal relevance is that it increases the student's ability to establish career plans thoughtfully. The disadvantaged student in particular, who has had limited contact with the broader society, is given opportunities to explore and chart new career paths. His vistas can be greatly expanded, and relationships with sectors of the community formerly unfamiliar to him are facilitated by cooperative education. These unusual aspects of educational relevance contribute to a reduction in rates of attrition (Lindenmeyer, 1966, and Smith, 1965).

One project objective of the five-college cooperative education consortium in California is to demonstrate cooperative education's effectiveness in recruiting and maintaining disadvantaged students. Their second annual report indicates that "retention of students is improved by a factor of nearly 2 to 1" (Bennett and Redding, 1972, pp. 1–2). In addition, San Mateo College, one of the five colleges, had demonstrated in an earlier study supported by the Ford Foundation that many potential dropouts remained in the program because of the particular benefits of the cooperative education program (Bennett, 1968 and 1970).

Another major contribution of cooperative education in serving disadvantaged students is to intensify the assimilation of students in the community power structure. In a very significant way, for those students who have been disenfranchised from the larger community (including handicapped students, see particularly Bennett and Redding's *Second Annual Report,* 1972, pp. 25–27), cooperative education is more than just the *promise* of participation in the affairs of the community after graduation, it is the immediate involvement in that process. It is an involvement that can stimulate a new concept of self and a revitalized notion of the student's relationship to the larger society. Jobs and education are combined in an important new partnership for changing the direction of the poor and disadvantaged (see especially McKinney in Knowles' *Handbook of Cooperative Education,* 1971, pp. 272–274).

Arthur Pearl and Frank Riessman in *New Careers for the Poor* (1965) observe: "The essence of poverty . . . is the scarcity of unskilled jobs. . . . In order to open the system to poor, jobs must be redefined to enable the unskilled, inexperienced, and uneducated to be eligible for employment in these areas. . . . Reduced to the simplicity of a slogan, new careers are a means to: obtain service from the poor in the place of providing service to the poor" (1965, pp. 21–22).

They offer a plan whereby the system might integrate the poor's particular skills in meaningful ways as a part of its ongoing function, dispensing with overly stringent job specifications. They comment on traditional patterns of employment as they relate to the poor: "Society insists that training takes place prior to job placement. Such a system made sense (although it reinforced inequality) when only a small percentage of the population was engaged in highly skilled occupations. . . . There can be no end to poverty unless it is fully appreciated that, for the most part, training for the poor must take place after employment is secured." They observe that the poor "must be permitted to play a useful, meaningful role in today's world. There can be no sacrifice of a population of today under the mantle of concern for tomorrow. Inability to deal with the poor of today will be transmitted to the poor of tomorrow" (1965, pp. 3–4). The *New Careers* advocacy is for dropping the "education before employment" requirement in favor of a commitment to employment followed by training to upgrade the employee in the career area. The cooperative education plan similarly recognizes that for many of the poor and disenfranchised, the promise of work after X number of years of college seems unrealistic and futile. Cooperative education departs from the *New Careers* plan by replacing the traditional education-then-work sequence with a merger of education and work.

Dr. Robert Bennett, assistant to the Chancellor, Superintendent for Resource Development, and Project Director of the San Mateo Junior College District, is outspoken in his support of the broad implications of the *New Careers* message for community college educators. San Mateo's evening cooperative program was called "new careers" to convey the kind of mission they envisioned for that endeavor. (The name was later changed so as not to be confused with the federally funded program having the same title. Dr. Bennett has presented his views on a combined system of cooperative education, coordinated technological instruction, student development, and articulated career-style model which has special implications for education of the disadvantaged in the March 1972 issue of *Junior College Journal*.) In addition to providing upgrading instruction for those already employed in satisfying positions, San Mateo attempts to work with community residents who are underemployed, offering retraining and where possible a job rotation program with their employers. The community college has the potential for "outreach" and the placement of disadvantaged citizens in meaningful work positions closely coordinated with a program of study. The college can make an important contribution to the solution of the problems of the community's poor, but the cooperation of the city's employers is fundamental to such a human development program. As to the difficulty of achieving this cooperation when students are disadvantaged and unskilled, Dawson observes: "Many employers have already responded to the need for hiring and training the hard-core unemployed. Employing cooperative students, who are part of a college program for educating students from poverty areas of our society, would have even greater appeal because of the college sharing in their supervision and training." Given the dimensions of this most critical national problem, Dawson recommends to college administrators that "even considerable risk would seem to be highly warranted" (1971, p. 15).

Although this book has dealt primarily with comprehensive community colleges, some specialized two-year college hybrids have made significant contributions. A new two-year college which is part of the New York City College System is practicing an unorthodox and fresh style of two-year college cooperative education within the framework of a single institutional mission. The College of Human Services was initially a private institution and the creation of Audrey Cohen, now the President of the College (*Time* Magazine, July 6, 1970). The college limits its enrollment to women residing in New York City who desire careers in the human services, who are 21 years or older, in good health, have the ability to read, write, and do basic arithmetic, and have poverty-level incomes as established by the U.S. Department of Labor. The curriculum of the college is taught by an interdisciplinary approach which includes psychology, urban affairs, sociology, education, and communication arts, in alternation with work in a service agency in the city. Basic skills are taught in the program because a high school degree is not a prerequisite for admission. For the first year, students receive an educational scholarship from the college. Second-year students, who are in the regular employ of an agency receive an annual salary from the agency; these students work three days and attend classes two days on a full-time basis, for which they are provided with a scholarship from the college (*New York Times,* October 29, 1970, and *National Observer,* April 13, 1970). The College of Human Services prepares students for careers as teacher asistants, social work assistants, occupational therapy assistants, community liaison trainees, community health assistants, recreational therapy assistants, and several others (A. C. Cohen, 1970). The comprehensive community college might advantageously study the cooperative program at the College for Human Services for augmentation in its own general studies or community service programs. The barriers to women in the community's social and economic institutions can be effectively penetrated through cooperative education. Stereotyped roles for women can be replaced with new, vital, and more meaningful careers as new opportunities for self-fulfillment are opened through cooperative education. (See particularly VanSickle in Knowles' *Handbook of Cooperative Education,* 1971, pp. 263–270, and Bennett and Redding's *Second Annual Report,* 1972, pp. 30–32.) The potential of cooperative education for penetrating employment barriers, improving self-concepts, suggesting career direction, and breaking down traditional occupational stereotypes for minorities and the poor also apply to women.

Lees Junior College in Kentucky pioneers in yet another area of service to the poor. Tom Noe at Lees Junior College directs an off-campus cooperative education program in addition to a special cooperative program called ALCOR, which is designed to place poor Appalachian youth enrolled at the college in the service of remote Appalachian communities. This program is offered in conjunction with Alice Lloyd College, Southeast Community College, and Cumberland College. Educational, health, and recreational services are provided by the Lees Junior College students during these work periods scheduled during the summer months. The students live with families in the area and operate programs from community centers and schools. Not only do the communities benefit from the participation of these college social servants, but the students gain skills and insights critical to their occupational goals (Lees Junior College Bulletin, 1971–1972, pp. 35–36).

In conclusion, community college cooperative education can creatively be adapted in any number of ways to provide especially valuable educational services to disadvantaged youth and adults of the community. In fact, implementation of a comprehensive cooperative education program in community colleges is strategic to the achievement of important educational values for all disadvantaged persons in the community.

The Challenge

★★
★★

This book has expressed the view that comprehensive cooperative education, designed for the unique philosophical, functional, and organizational parameters of the community college, is the single best hope for intensifying the "community" aspects of community college education. It should be clear by now that cooperative education can provide significant educational benefits to everyone; it is hoped that this book has effectively suggested how community college educators can allocate their resources in order to provide a qualitatively superior education.

Six important challenges now confront community college cooperative educators. The first challenge is to fashion a style of cooperative education that is suited to the distinct institutional mission of the community college. Practices in cooperative vocational education and the general form of cooperative education in liberal arts colleges and universities reveal a rich pattern of cooperative education philosophy and operation, but it is incumbent on community college educators to forge a uniquely community college style of cooperative education—a style supportive of its own function

161

and philosophy. The third, fourth, and sixth challenges discussed below suggest possible nuances of this style.

The second challenge is to foster a revitalized concept of the employer in the cooperative education program, and this challenge is contingent upon the employer's acceptance of two large responsibilities. The first of these is to participate more actively in the educational aspects of the program. The employer should be encouraged to direct his firm's resources, including its managerial talents, to the accomplishment of the educational role implied by the title of training supervisor. It is not expected that employers will subvert their primary economic goals in order to do this; but cooperative education is an educational program first, last, and foremost, and it cannot be fully successful without the contributions of sympathetic, knowledgeable, and educationally sensitive supervisors. Progress will be made in this area when employers are clearly informed of the important benefits cooperative education can contribute to the student, the community, and the firm when sufficient support is given to the educational thrust of the program. The second responsibility—which is more difficult to accept because it requires a greater change in attitude and a larger commitment of resources on the part of the employer—is for the employer to contribute actively to the administration of the program, so that it can become truly community-centered. A model for such a plan already exists in the Career Advancement Program, or CAP, of Rock Valley College, a two-year school in Rockford, Illinois. Under the Rock Valley plan, participating companies share recruitment, selection, placement, coordination, and promotional phases of the cooperative education program with the college. This program is an outstanding example of the kind of institutional participation and involvement that employers can make, and it has important implications for every community college offering a cooperative education program (Hallstrom, 1968, pp. 120–121, and the Rock Valley College CAP, 1968, pp. 1–23).

The third major challenge facing community college educators is to commit themselves to a strategic as opposed to a tactical view of cooperative education. Community college cooperative education cannot be successful unless administrative leaders firmly support the program's values and are willing to provide the resources

necessary to the fulfillment of its objectives. It is argued in the pre-
ceding pages that this commitment might ideally extend to the
implementation of a comprehensive cooperative education program
with work experience provided to students in all program areas, and
that if feasible it be provided on a mandatory basis. Such a strategic
conception, as opposed to a tactical application in limited program
areas, can spread the benefits of cooperative education to the widest
possible clientele.

The fourth challenge, which is discussed more completely in
Chapter Eight is the challenge of implementing a defined-outcomes
methodology in cooperative education to foster a student or "product" orientation, as opposed to a process orientation. Historically,
the development of new systems, whether in the industrial, political,
or educational realms, begins with a heavy process-orientation that
tends to shift toward a product orientation as the system is per-
fected. Systems evaluated on their need-satisfying ability must of
necessity be product-oriented. In the industrial sector, consumer
goods must be fashioned to please the consumer, not the production
manager; firms preoccupied with subtleties of operational procedure, engineering detail, and product performance in the laboratory,
to the exclusion of the consumer, may suffer the penalties of failure
in the market place. The same is true in education. Cooperative
education must reflect an institutional commitment to serve student
needs, not a fascination on the part of educators with the details
of process. It is crucial that community college cooperative educators focus on a procedure for specifying desired learning outcomes
from work experiences—rather than assuming learning on the job
occurs by osmosis. To facilitate such a change in perspective, the
defined-outcome approach whereby student outcomes are specified
and measured ought to become an integral part of the cooperative
education activity (in both micro and macro senses, see Chapter
Eight).

The fifth challenge is to carry out a systematic research effort
to measure the success with which the cooperative effort supplies
educational values. Data indicating lower attrition, improved academic performance, and higher wages for cooperative students when
compared with non-cooperative students are important findings;
but much more needs to be discovered about student learning and

career development, the assimilation of disadvantaged students in the larger society, the passage of community college levies, student attitudes toward work, education, and other variables, and various employer perceptions about training, student performance, and educational parameters of cooperative programs. The identification of strategic areas for research might logically be made by associations of vocational, cooperative, or community-college educators. Such a program should include a systematic national plan and a grassroots effort based in the institutional research activities of individual community colleges.

The sixth and final challenge confronting community college administrators is to give careful thought to cooperative education's pertinent relationships to the community dimension of its philosophy—to demonstrate institutional commitment to a truly new form of education—an unconventional but qualitatively superior education with the capability of providing important benefits for community, employers, and students.

The reason for a merger between cooperative education and the community college is the provision of important service to the needs of people. The separatism and occasional divisiveness which have long characterized the relationship between "town and gown" are ready to give way to a harmonious partnership in the service of community need. The lines of demarcation between the human endeavors of education and work can and should be diminished—and the "community" college, in particular, by virtue of its philosophical and operational patterns, is in a position to bring about such a reorientation.

★★★★★★★★★★★★ A ★★★★★★★★★★★★
★★★★★★★★★★★★   ★★★★★★★★★★★★

A Cooperative
Education Report
and Record System

★★★★★★★★★★★★★★★★★★★★★★★★★★★★★★★★★★★★
★★★★★★★★★★★★★★★★★★★★★★★★★★★★★★★★★★★★

1. SAMPLE COVER LETTER FOR STUDENT SURVEY:

COOPERATIVE EDUCATION COMMUNITY COLLEGE

Dear Community Resident:

Cooperative Education Community College is interested in knowing more about you—your career ambitions, personal development needs, and educational requirements. The college is continually trying to provide educationally relevant programs that will serve a broad range of community needs by a merging of on-campus and off-campus experiences.

Your response to this questionnaire will aid the college in this mission.

Sincerely,

Director of Cooperative Education

Enclosure: Questionnaire
            Stamped Return Envelope

2.   SAMPLE SURVEY OF PROSPECTIVE STUDENTS:

1. Do you plan to attend college in the next year? Yes.............. No.............

2. If yes, check the primary purpose of your plan for collegiate study. Career preparation.............. Personal development............. Career upgrading in present job............. Exploration............. Undecided............. If other, please indicate...

3. What are your important interests and hobbies? ....
   ....
   ....

4. Do you presently work? Yes.............. No.............. (If no, answer Question Five)
   If Yes, indicate if work is Part-time............. Full-time............. And
   Name of Firm ....
   Job title ....

5. Have you participated in high school or other collegiate cooperative education programs? Yes............. No.............
   If yes, indicate school ....
   If yes, indicate cooperative employer ....

6. Have you worked in other positions? Yes............. No............. (If no, answer Question Seven)
   Please List Employer(s) and date(s) worked (List most recent positions first) ....
   ....
   ....

7. Are you familiar with your local community college's cooperative education program? Yes............. No............. (If no, answer Question Eight)
   If yes, how?...

8. Would you like to receive more information? Yes............. No...........
   If yes, supply name and address ....
   ....
   ....

   NOTE: Please return this questionnaire in the enclosed return envelope, or return it to the college representative if the questionnaire is administered on location.

3. SAMPLE COMMUNITY SURVEY COVER LETTER:

COOPERATIVE EDUCATION COMMUNITY COLLEGE

Dear Mr. (Employer):

Cooperative Education Community College is committed
to a comprehensive cooperative education program for all
of its students wherein classroom instruction and paid work
experience related to the student's educational needs are
combined in a unique partnership of community and
college. Community institutions receive the benefit of a
trained manpower pool and students gain a qualitatively
superior education.

The college is conducting a survey to determine the number
of community institutions which would be able to provide
paid employment to Cooperative Education Community
College students. Will you please complete the enclosed
questionnaire and return it in the stamped, addressed
envelope provided?

Your participation in this survey will add to the effectiveness of the college's planning for this program. Thank you
for your assistance.

Sincerely,

Director of Cooperative
Education

Enclosure: Questionnaire
Stamped Return Envelope

4. SAMPLE COMMUNITY SURVEY:

The information provided from this survey will not be used for purposes other than college use.

Name of organization...

Character of activity provided by the organization....................................

....

Number of person employed....................................

   Part-time employees.....................................

   Full-time employees.....................................

How many college students does your firm now employ?.........................

Are part-time workers required by your firm during any particular time of the year (if yes, check those that apply)

Summers ( ) Weekends ( ) Christmas ( )

Other times ( )

Specify: ....

....

What are your sources for the recruitment of new employees? (You may check more than one)

   High school recruitment   ....

   Two-year college recruitment ....

   University recruitment   ....

   Employment agencies   ....

   Voluntary applications   ....

   Others (specify)...

If you do employ college students which major or course areas do you prefer them to have studied? (You may check more than one)

   Traditional liberal arts ....

   Human services   ....

   Engineering   ....

   Business and commerce ....

   Allied health   ....

   No preference   ....

   Others (specify)...

Areas of employment shortages...

....

....

Areas of anticipated employment reduction...

....

....

WHAT ARE TYPICAL ENTRY-LEVEL OR BEGINNING POSITIONS FOR COMMUNITY COLLEGE STUDENTS?

Describe. ....

....

....

What is the most serious training problem confronting your firm?

....

....

What major changes in your firm's technology or operation do you envision in the future?..

....

....

How would this affect employment?...

....

....

Please briefly describe your firm's training program, if any.................

....

....

....

Were you familiar with Cooperative Education Community College's commitment to a cooperative education program prior to this survey?

          Yes............ No............

Has your firm participated in a cooperative education program with other schools or colleges?

          Yes............ No............

Do you favor a collegiate program which provides an integral program of work experience in conjunction with classroom studies in serving our community's educational needs?

          Yes............ No............

Would your firm be interested in cooperating with the college in providing work experience for community college students?

          Yes, my firm is interested and we would like more information. ....

          No, your training program has no application for my firm. ....

Name and title of company official completing this survey.

Telephone Number

5. SAMPLE STUDENT INFORMATION FORM:

1. Name.. Age.....................

2. Birthdate.............................. Sex.............. Today's date.......................

3. Home address...
   Telephone...............................

4. Marital Status.. Number of children..............

5. If you are single do you live with your family? Yes............
   No............ If no, where do you live?...

6. Physical limitations: Yes............ No............ Specify...........................
   ....

7. Father's occupation and place of employment.................................
   ....

8. Mother's occupation and place of employment...............................
   ....

9. What is your family's income classification? Please check one.
   0—$4,999   ....
   $5,000—7,499   ....
   $7,500—9,999   ....
   $10,000—14,999   ....
   $15,000—19,999   ....
   $20,000 and over   ....

10. Are you a veteran? Yes............ No............ Specify service...................
    .... Selective Service Number.............................

11. Where did you graduate from high school?.................................
    .... When?...............................

12. Were you in a cooperative education program in high school?
    Yes............ No............ Where did you work? Dates?.......................
    ....

13. What other colleges have you attended? Dates?.............................
....

14. Were you in a cooperative education program at the college? Where did you work? Dates? ....

15. When do you plan to enroll in the career orientation class? .... When do you plan to enroll in a work period?...

16. What are your career or educational goals?.................................
....

17. What are your strongest personal skills? Indicate areas of strength by use of numerical values: 5 (very strong) through 0 (absence of skill).
Social skills (strong people-orientation)............
Technical skills (concern for detail)............
Conceptual skills (thinking and philosophizing about the meaning of things)............

18. What is it that you would like most to do or be in the next five years?...
ten years?..

19. Do you own a car?............ Do you have use of a car?...................

20. Hobbies or interests...

21. Did you receive any honors or awards while in high school or college? Yes............ No............ If yes, please list.......................
....
....

22. What social or community organizations do you belong to?
....
....

23. Are you currently employed? Yes............ No............ If yes, please complete the following:

24. Name of firm.. Phone......................

25. Address ....
     (specify division or department)

     ....

26. Work supervisor's name...
     Title..

27. Your job title.. Number of hours
     per week...

28. Brief job description...

     ....

29. Hourly rate.. Do you wish to work here for
     your cooperative work period? Yes............. No............. Has it been
     approved by the coop department? Yes............. No.............

30. If no, indicate your rationale for its approval (in light of
     educational and career objectives)...

     ....

     ....

31. Do you plan to attend college year-round? Yes............. No.............
     If no, which quarters will you miss?...

32. If you plan to be away from campus this summer, specify
     location ....

     ....

33. What type of work would you like to have during your
     cooperative work period?..

     ....

34. Indicate rationale (in light of educational and career
     objectives) ....

     ....

     ....

     ....

6. SAMPLE SYLLABUS FOR CAREER ORIENTATION
    CLASS (two credit hours for two contact hours a week):

Objectives: You should be able to clarify important avocational
and vocational interests and capabilities important to job success,
identify and be familiar with sources of occupational information
and statistics, set forth career and educational objectives and a
plan of work and study to achieve them, and to demonstrate skills
in interviewing, preparing data sheets, and in human relations and
communications.

Course Schedule:

Date	Class Theme
1st week	Cooperative education: history and values; overview of course.
2nd week	Administration of vocational aptitiude and interest tests.
3rd week	Occupational and education spectrums; sources of secondary data on career opportunities and how to locate them.
4th week	Human relations and its significance in successful employment; case studies.
5th week	Preparing the data sheet and letter of application.
6th week	Interpretation of test results; how to carry off an effective interview with a prospective employer.
7th week	Interview with personnel director (on closed circuit television).
8th week	Presentations by students currently co-oping concerning their experiences on the job.
9th week	Cooperative education procedures; how to make the most of your cooperative education experience.
10th week	Field trips to numerous public and private agencies (term paper due).
11th week	Examination; final lectures

Evaluation:

1. Final examination	25%
2. Participation in interview situations, case studies, and class discussion	25%
3. Term paper on your career and personal objectives	25%
4. Written assignments (data sheets, letters of introduction, and other periodic short reports)	25%

7. SAMPLE CARD OF STUDENT INTRODUCTION TO
    THE COMPANY:

ADDRESS ON FRONT OF CARD:

Cooperative Education Community College
Department of Cooperative Education
Experiential Avenue
City

TEXT ON REVERSE OF CARD:

Dear Mr. .... :

...., a student at the Cooperative
Education Community College majoring in .... is
here to interview for a student trainee position with your firm under
the partnership arrangement with the college. He is able to start work
beginning the date of .... The team member
who will alternate with this student is..

At the completion of the interview will you please complete the
following and mail immediately.

Student was hired............ Starting date.................................
Student was not acceptable, please send additional students...........................

Date within the first two weeks of starting date when the three of us
can establish learning objectives:...
Comments: ....

Sincerely,

Cooperative Coordinator

8. SAMPLE LEARNING OUTCOME AND TRAINING AGREEMENT FORM (three-part form for student, employer, and coordinator):

COOPERATIVE EDUCATION COMMUNITY COLLEGE
Statement of Work Period Defined Outcomes

For .... at ....
        (student's name)   (employer)

on ....
      (today's date)

Cooperative education is a valid learning experience to the degree that the college provides adequate training and guidance, the employer provides supervision, and the student sets about the task of understanding and managing the nature of his work. But moreover, cooperative education is educationally valid to the extent that learning outcomes can be specifically defined and measured for each student trainee. On the following lines specify the objectives for this work period. At the end of the quarter both the student and employer will evaluate the achievement of the objectives in the space given to the right via a satisfactory (S) or unsatisfactory (U) rating.

At the completion of the work experience period the student should be able to:

Evaluation of Achievement of Objective

STUDENT   EMPLOYER

1. ....

....

....

2. ....

....

....

3. ....

....

....

Evaluation of Achievement
of Objective

STUDENT   EMPLOYER

4. ....

....

5. ....

....

Qualifying Comments: ....

....

TRAINING AGREEMENT: The validity of the defined outcomes and the responsibilities of each of the cooperative education
participants are secured by the signatures below. *The Student* will
adhere to all policies of the employing firm; will report to work
promptly, and in the event of illness or emergency will notify the
employer and coordinator promptly; will direct his energies to the
completion of work assignments; and will not terminate employment without first meeting with the coordinator. *The Employer*
will recognize the student as a trainee and to that end will provide
varied experiences and adequate supervision; will assure safe and
healthful working conditions; will offer wages comparable to
existing wage rates for the student's job; will, if for any reason
termination of employment is necessary, meet with both student
and coordinator in a special meeting; and will agree not to hire
the student on a full-time basis during the student's tenure of
study at the college. *The College* will provide instruction concurrent with the work assignment which examines desirable job
attitudes and skills, will periodically visit the student and the
employer to ascertain progress in the student's work, will provide
guidance for special student problems, and will grant college credit
toward the completion of the student's degree.

Employer ....

Student ....

Coordinator ....

9.   SAMPLE COORDINATOR VISITATION REPORT

1. Employer visited... Date................................

2. Address ....

   Telephone ....

3. Student Employee ....

4. Job Title or function..

5. Interview with student:

   Yes............ No............

   With employer:

   Yes............ No............

6. Supervisor's name.. Title..................

7. Purpose of visitation..

8. Observations concerning student..

   ....

9. Observations concerning employer..

   ....

   ....

10. Implications ....

   ....

   ....

11. Optimum time to call (day and hour)...

12. Suggested time and date for next call...

10. SAMPLE WEEKLY VISITATION REPORT FILED BY
    COORDINATOR

Coordinator's Name.. Week of.........................

Date	Company visited	Address	Title	Length	Purpose of Visit

Student Conferences		Employer Conferences	
Monday	....	Monday	....
Tuesday	....	Tuesday	....
Wednesday	....	Wednesday	....
Thursday	....	Thursday	....
Friday	....	Friday	....
Total	....	Total	....

Students working...

Students not working...

Total Students...

* Students not yet assigned learning objectives.....................................

** Defined outcome forms not yet picked up for evaluation...........

Coordinator's signature...

* Answer the 2nd and 3rd weeks of class only
** Answer the 10th and 11th weeks of class only

11. SAMPLE COORDINATOR EXPENSE ACCOUNT RECORD

Coordinator's Name.. Date...............................

Summary of Expenditures

       I.   Automobile travel in personally owned
           cars (mi. x .10)   ....

      II. Travel and fares (specify means)   ....

           (List destination and total miles traveled

           for I and II on reverse side)

     III. Meals (specify where)

                Breakfast   ....

                Lunch   ....

                Dinner   ....

     IV. Hotel room (specify where)   ....

      V. Telephone Calls (specify where)   ....

    VI. Miscellaneous   ....

           Total Expenses   ....

NOTE: Attach all receipts for expenses incurred and list expenses not categorized above on a separate sheet of paper

12.   SAMPLE STUDENT—COORDINATOR INTERVIEW
      FORM:

Name of Student... Date............................

Work Station.. Work Periods

Completed...

Coopportunity Cluster... Expected

Graduation..

Purpose of Meeting...

Comments ....

....

....

....

....

....

....

....

....

....

....

....

....

Rating*	Rationale
Appearance	
Communications Skill	
Courtesy	
Warmth of Personality	
Friendliness	
Self-Confidence	
Employability	

* 1—good
  2—average
  3—weak

13. SAMPLE WORK PROFILE FILED BY STUDENT AT END OF WORK PERIOD

    1. Name.. Today's date............................

        Date you began work this quarter..

    2. Home address...

        Telephone..

    3. Career or educational objective..

        ....

        ....

    4. Coopportunity Cluster enrolled in..

    5. Place of employment...

        Department..

    6. Job description...
                             (specify your title)

        ....

        ....

    7. Name of work supervisor................................ Title................................

    8. Address of employer..

        Telephone..

    9. Working hours and days of week...

        Rate of pay.................................... Total hours worked........................

   10. Career practicum you are enrolled in this quarter..........................

        ....Time and days of week................................

   11. Have you completed the career orientation class? Yes.................

        No............ Date completed..

12. Name of team member who alternates cooperative periods with you..

13. What is your approximate grade point average to date?............

14. Number of credit hours to complete the degree................................

15. This is my 1st............ 2nd............ 3rd............ 4th............ work experience quarter

16. Was this work experience quarter educationally or personally rewarding? Yes............ No............ Why?................................

17. What can your employer or cooperative coordinator do to make your next work periods more educationally rewarding?

....

....

18. Important: This must be mailed or left in the office of your cooperative coordinator prior to..

                                                              (date)

....

Signature   Social Security Number

14. SAMPLE EMPLOYER PROMOTIONAL LETTER:
COOPERATIVE EDUCATION COMMUNITY COLLEGE

Dear Sirs:

The introduction of practical work experiences into college students' programs of study is an important educational innovation of this community college; it is a tested and demonstrably effective program, which has been practiced since 1906 at the University of Cincinnati and in many other institutions of higher learning. It is an educationally superior program which provides a career orientation for all of our students, acquainting them with the realities of work, and allowing them to "test out" classroom theories and concepts.

This unique partnership of community and college is based on certain overwhelming advantages of integrating college and community resources. The college is revitalized and refreshed. The ivory tower concept is deflated. Students receive a quality of education heretofore not available. But what about the community, and specifically your firm?

Should you decide to become a partner with the college in the creation of an educationally superior program, there can be important advantages for your firm. Specifically, the program provides your firm with:

—A pool of college-trained community residents for your long-range employment needs
—Student trainees, who are evaluated by the college and receive credit for their work experience and who are capable of efficiently and effectively meeting certain of your short-term employment needs
—An on-going training program which the college will attempt to individualize to your needs, making it available to your current employees (and counting their work experiences toward filling the requirements of the program)
—An opportunity to provide a socially responsible service to the community (such as providing relevant education for minority and poor students and all community inhabitants)

Would you be willing to participate with the college by hiring a team or teams of eager, trained students who are committed to the educational values of work and thus to the achievement of your firm's objectives? If you would like additional information and a chance to talk with a staff member about this program, then mail the enclosed pre-paid, addressed postcard today. Thank you.

                     Sincerely,
                     Director of Cooperative Education

Enclosure: Return Postcard

15. SAMPLE LETTER TO RECRUIT COOPERATIVE EDUCATION ADVISORY COMMITTEE MEMBERS

COOPERATIVE EDUCATION COMMUNITY COLLEGE

Dear Mr. ....:

It is with great pleasure that we invite you to participate in the Cooperative Education Community College's cooperative education advisory committee. Your appointment, should you accept, has been approved by the Board of Trustees of the Community College District for a period of three years.

Because of your acknowledged expertise as a practitioner, the college looks forward to the potentially important contributions that you can make to the cooperative education program. Your input is essential to the development of community orientation and the formulation of objecives, policies, and procedures for the program.

The first meeting of the committee will be held in room .... on .... at .... in order to
                   (date)   (time)
consider the broad aims of the cooperative education program and the function and authority of this committee. The agenda for the meeting is enclosed.

Sincerely,

President

Enclosure: Agenda

16.　SAMPLE OUTLINE OF STUDENT HANDBOOK:

1. Welcome to a new style of community college education which merges study and work experience.

2. History and philosophy of cooperative education

3. Cooperative education's relationship to your educational objectives (coopportunity clusters)

4. How the program operates

5. Calendar

6. Absence from work, dismissal

7. Social Security and work laws

8. Career placement class

9. Placement on the job

10. Defined-outcomes approach

11. Training agreement

12. Career practicum class

13. Requirements for career practicum report

14. Evaluation of defined outcomes

15. End of work period form

16. Work experience evaluation: achievement of objectives and practicum outcomes

17. SAMPLE STUDENT FOLLOW-UP COVER LETTER:

COOPERATIVE EDUCATION COMMUNITY COLLEGE

Dear Mr. or Ms. ....:

The Cooperative Education Community College, in order to continually upgrade its cooperative education program, attempts to keep in contact with former students in order to find out what they are doing and to encourage their suggestions for improving the cooperative education program. To help the college in this regard, will you kindly fill in the attached questionnaire?

Please clearly indicate your answers on the enclosed questionnaire and mail it promptly to the college in the enclosed stamped and addressed envelope. Your responses will be kept entirely confidential. Your cooperation in providing the college with this information is greatly appreciated.

Sincerely,

Director of Cooperative Education

Enclosures: Stamped Return
Envelope

18. SAMPLE STUDENT FOLLOW-UP QUESTIONNAIRE:

Name.. Date............................

Address ....

Sex............ Marital Status............................ Number of Children............

Maiden Name...

1. Did you transfer to another college or university after graduation? Yes............ No............ If so, where did you transfer to? .... What was your major?.. When did or will you graduate?................ What was your coopportunity cluster and major at CECC?..

2. Are you employed by a firm in which you co-oped with as a student at CECC? Yes............ No............ If yes, what is the firm? ....

3. If no, who is your present employer?...................................... What is your job title and responsibility there?.....................

....

....

Salary? ....

4. List employment you have had since graduation, beginning with the most recent position and moving backward in time

Employer	Job Title	Dates	Salary	Reason for Leaving

5. Are you employed full-time in your present position? Yes............ No............ Did you purposely seek out that employment because of a personal or family need? Yes............ No............ If yes, what is that need..

....

6. Are your current personal needs and goals similar to those you experienced as a student? Yes............. No.............. If no, why? ....

....

7. Do you believe you were hired because of your CECC education?
   Yes............. No.............
   If yes, what aspect of your college education was a primary influence in your employment?...

....

8. Do you feel your cooperative education was important to your job success? Why? How?...

....

9. Which courses and work experiences were most valuable to you in your process of career development?...................................

....

10. If you could have changed your program of study in any way, what would you have done?...

....

....

11. If cooperative education had been optional and you were to do it all over again, would you have selected the program? Yes............. No.............

12. Additional comments or recommendations..

....

....

....

★★★★★★★★★★★★★★ B ★★★★★★★★★★★★★★
★★★★★★★★★★★★★★ ★★★★★★★★★★★★★★

Sample Cooperative Education Report Requirements

★★★★★★★★★★★★★★★★★★★★★★★★★★★★★★★★★★★★
★★★★★★★★★★★★★★★★★★★★★★★★★★★★★★★★★★★★

1. LETTER STATING REQUIREMENTS FOR REPORTS BY COOPERATIVE EDUCATION STUDENTS:

BOROUGH OF MANHATTAN COMMUNITY COLLEGE
THE CITY UNIVERSITY OF NEW YORK

Dear Cooperative Education Student:

Part of your Cooperative Education assignment each semester is a written report. The purpose of this is to allow you to use the experience and knowledge you have gained as a Cooperative Education intern to analyze, interpret, and evaluate situations which are similar to those you might encounter throughout your vocational and occupational career.

Your topic is listed below. You should answer only those questions which have been assigned to you by the code below. Read the code completely and carefully and proceed to the appropriate question(s). Write a paper 750 words long, approximately three (3) typewritten pages. Your paper should be typewritten and double-spaced. Handwritten papers are acceptable only if they are legible and double-spaced. Each paper must be accompanied by a cover sheet.

The cover sheet must include the following:

> Name
>
> Social Security Number
>
> Major
>
> Course Code Number
>
> Name of topic
>
> Your Coordinator's name

All papers are due no later than Friday, May 5, 1972. Be sure to make at least one copy of your paper.

If you wish to mail your paper, it should be addressed to:

> Your Coordinator
> Cooperative Education Department—A 340
> Manhattan Community College
> 134 West 51st Street
> New York, N. Y. 10020

		Question(s) *to be done*
Question Code		
First internship students *only*	(2 credits)	Question 1 *or* 2 *or* 3
Students registered for one internship *other than their first* internship	(2 credits)	Question 2 *or* 3
Students registered for 2 internships	(4 credits)	Question 2 *and* 3

(1) One of the objectives of the Cooperative Education internship is to help students make long-range career plans. The student, for example, may have an experience which confirms his career choice for him. On the other hand, the student may find aspects of the field which are not compatible with either his interests or his personality. The student may also find that he prefers working in a large firm to a small firm, or that he prefers a firm with clear lines of authority and responsiblity as opposed to one where relations are informal. In this term paper, please discuss what you have learned in your current assignment which may influence jobs you will take in the future.

(2) Very often, students who are doing internships, especially their first, find that a certain adjustment is necessary before they feel comfortable at their jobs. Sometimes a heavy school-work load, poor study habits, a difficult home situation, a bad experience on the job during the first few weeks, or even a personality conflict with someone at the job can make the adjustment period difficult. Sometimes the adjustment is not possible for various reasons and the completion of the internship for that semester is delayed until later when perhaps the problems have been worked out. Please discuss the above statements, bringing into context any adjustment problems you feel you may have experienced at times and how they affected your productivity at work. Feel free to be as specific as you wish in describing problems you have encountered. Then discuss how, if you were in management's position, you would have handled a person such as yourself, experiencing a difficult adjustment period because of various problems, be they at home, school or elsewhere. (If you have not experienced adjustment problems, please discuss this question in relation to others you have observed.)

(3) One of the key facets in the way any firm operates is its management of personnel, that is, the quality and amount of supervision; the incentives for good work (both financial and psychological for example, compliments, recognition); the overall climate set by management and related attitudes of employees. In this term paper, please discuss the way the employees are managed in the firm in which you are interning. Describe this in detail, indicating your opinion of the quality of personnel management. If you consider the situation lacking in some respect, indicate what change you would try to bring about.

If you have any questions, please contact your coordinator at the Cooperative Education Office, A 340, as soon as possible.

Respectfully yours,

Dean, Cooperative Education
and Community Relations

2. EXCERPTS FROM THE SINCLAIR COMMUNITY
    COLLEGE INTERNSHIP CONTRACT:

> *A Report Form Developed by Jim Puthoff and Barry
> Heermann of Sinclair Community College, Incorporat-
> ing Requirements of Distributive Education Reports
> Advocated by Neal Vivian, Teacher-Educator, Distribu-
> tive Education, Ohio State University.*

Requirements for the .... Program
include at least three quarters of directed, on-the-job experience
under the supervision of ...., co-op
coordinator, and in consultation with ....,
coordinator of your program.

Students enrolling in this program have three quarters of paid
employment in an occupation directly related to your educational
goals. Such employment will be in positions in (list illustrative
work cites) ....
....

For each quarter of full-time employment the student may
enroll in four credit hours of internship credit for a minimum of
twelve quarter hours (accumulated during the fourth, sixth, and
eighth quarters for most students).

In every instance the proposed employment must be approved
in advance by the coordinator of cooperative education.

A grade will be given for each internship based upon a written
assignment to be turned in no later than Monday of the tenth
week of the quarter or at the date specified by a coordinator. The
internship report must be typed and double spaced, with a title
page specifying the grade for which the student has contracted
and the internship for which the student has registered. Copies
of this report must be submitted to *both* your advisor and the
coop coordinator. A contract grade system based on a sequence of
student objectives will be used.

INTERNSHIP I, UNIT REQUIREMENTS:

(The First of Three Internship Contracts)

PREREQUISITE: Two quarters of full-time study including the following coursework (specify) :...

SHOULD YOU DESIRE AN A:

TASK 1: You should develop a written narrative job description of the duties you perform in your capacity during this internship period.

Condition: Consult with your work supervisor and examine the "Narrative Job Description" materials attached. Given an indication in the description as to what degree this responsibility conforms or does not conform to your career objectives.

Criterion: Must be eight pages, double-spaced, typed.

TASK 2: You should describe twelve "critical incidents" you have encountered this internship period (a "critical incident" is a particularly effective or ineffective application of a work task).

Condition: The critical incidents must apply to *your* performance during the present internship period. See the sample critical incident form attached.

Criterion: Must be typed using the blank critical incident form attached, which you may wish to photocopy, citing twelve critical incidents (i.e., twelve pages).

SHOULD YOU DESIRE A B:

TASK 1: You should develop a written narrative job description of the duties you perform in your capacity this internship period.

Condition: Consult with your work supervisor and examine the "Narrative Job Description" materials attached. Give an indication in the description as to what degree this responsibility conforms or does not conform to your career objectives.

Criterion: Must be six pages, double-spaced, typed.

TASK 2: You should describe six "critical incidents" you have encountered this internship period (a "critical incident" is a particularly effective or ineffective application of a work task).

Condition: The critical incidents must apply to your performance the present internship period. See the sample critical incident form attached.

Criterion: Must be typed using the blank critical incident form attached, which you may wish to photocopy, citing six critical incidents (i.e., six pages).

SHOULD YOU DESIRE A C:

TASK 1: You should write a short report specifying what insights you have gained about yourself and your career objective having completed this internship period.

Condition: You should be honest with yourself and talk it over with your work supervisor.

Criterion: Must be three pages, typed, double-spaced.

TASK 2: You should write a job description and job specification for your present work responsibility.

Condition: The job description should clarify the range of tasks for which you are responsible, and the job specification should outline knowledge, skills, desired education levels, and experience required. Discuss this with your work supervisor.

Criterion: Two pages for the job description and two pages for the job specification, typed double-spaced.

★★★★★★★★★★★★★ C ★★★★★★★★★★★★★
★★★★★★★★★★★★★   ★★★★★★★★★★★★★

Cooperative Education Financial Planning Checklist

★★★★★★★★★★★★★★★★★★★★★★★★★★★★★★★★★★★★★★
★★★★★★★★★★★★★★★★★★★★★★★★★★★★★★★★★★★★★★

1. Determine the expected enrollments each year while the program is being installed and when it reaches full operation. (Enrollment figures are needed in order to know just how many placement opportunities must be provided.)

2. Decide on tuition and fees to be charged and calculate the total income during each of the years of conversion to cooperative education.

3. Determine additional faculty required to teach additional students and added faculty compensation (including fringe benefits) resulting from adoption of the plan.

4. Calculate the added costs of administration and clerical personnel.

5. Determine costs of coordination and placement—that is, costs of running a department of cooperative education.

6. Calculate other expenses, including additional costs of general and academic administration—deans of academic programs, registrar's office, computer services, additional library expenses, additional student services expenses, extra costs of financial aid, and changes in general expenses—catalogs, admissions office expenses, and added costs of maintenance.

7. Estimate planning and conversion costs and develop a model of income and expenses showing preconversion income and expenses, changes during each year of conversion to cooperative education, and the projected post-conversion income and expenses.

8. Post-conversion expenses
   A. Salaries
   B. Office expenses
   C. Telephone and telegraph
   D. Printing (handbooks, forms, newsletters)
   E. Travel and entertainment
   F. Staff training and development
   G. Memberships, conferences, and subscriptions to publications
   H. Social Security, Major Medical, group life insurance, and unemployment insurance
   I. Overhead (total administration and overhead costs assigned to department based on allocated space used)

Abstracted from Knowles and Wooldridge, 1971, pp. 293–294, 301–302.

★★★★★★★★★★★★★ D ★★★★★★★★★★★★★
★★★★★★★★★★★★★ ★★★★★★★★★★★★★

California
Community College
Cooperative Education
Consortium

Goals, Progress Report, and Objectives Form

★★★★★★★★★★★★★★★★★★★★★★★★★★★★★★★★★
★★★★★★★★★★★★★★★★★★★★★★★★★★★★★★★★★

199

1. GOALS (Bennett and Redding, 1971)

   1. To establish a substantial *national demonstration model.*

   2. To demonstrate the effectiveness of *alternate semester, parallel, and extended-day plans.*

   3. To prove the effectiveness of *recruiting, development, and coordination procedures* planned for a consortium effort of five California community colleges enrolling 1,000 cooperative education students.

   4. To prove the effectiveness of vocational cooperative education in *recruiting and maintaining disadvantaged students.*

   5. To demonstrate the effectiveness of vocational cooperative education in solving the *technical, business, and para-professional manpower recruiting and training problems* of business and industry.

2. PROGRESS REPORT (Bennett and Redding, 1972)

   1. A total of 3,095 students participated, over three times the 1,000 expected and planned for in the first year. Over 500 employees were involved in the program.

   2. Students reports consistently speak of the educational advantages of increased learning and better understanding of concepts that result from combining studies with on-the-job paid work experience in a chosen career field.

   3. Co-op students generally worked about 30 hours per week, earning an average of $2.64 per hour during 40 weeks for a *total combined earning in excess of eight million dollars.* Cooperative education has proved to be the largest financial support program existing at the colleges.

   4. Significant impact was made on the recruitment and retention of the disadvantaged through cooperative education.

200

3.   ORANGE COAST COLLEGE COOPERATIVE EDUCATION LEARNING OBJECTIVES FORM

Date ....

Employer ....

Student's Name ....

STATEMENT OF JOB-ORIENTED LEARNING OBJECTIVES

Each semester that a student is enrolled in the Cooperative Education Program it is necessary that the college help the student determine what new or expanded responsibilities or learning opportunities are possible on his job. These objectives enable us to determine the units of credit that will be granted for work experience.

These objectivs should be specific and measurable. They will be reviewed with the supervisor. At the end of the semester the student-employee and the supervisor will be asked to evaluate the level of attainment of each objective.

(1) ....

(2) ....

(3) ....

(4) ....

(5) ....

End-of-Term Rating

	Student	*Supervisor*
(1)		
(2)		
(3)		
(4)		
(5)		

Rating Scale
for Accomplishments

1 = Limited
2 = Average
3 = Better than average
4 = Far exceeds average

AGREEMENT

We the undersigned agree with the validity of the learning objectives listed above. The employer and the college agree to provide the necessary supervision and counseling to insure that the maximum educational benefit may be achieved for the employee-student's work experience.

There are three participants in the Cooperative Education venture. The student agrees to abide by the Cooperative Education guidelines. The supervisor will evaluate the employee-student's job performance at the end of the grading period. The college will award academic credit for work successfully accomplished.

....
Student's Signature   Supervisor's Signature

....
Instructor-Coordinator   Director

Distribution:
Pink: Office of Cooperative Education. *Gold:* Employer. *Yellow:* Student.
White: Rated at end-of-term to Office of Cooperative Education.

Bibliography

★★
★★

American Vocational Association. *Definition of Terms in Vocational and Practical Arts Education.* Washington, D.C.: Division of Vocational and Technical Education, U.S. Office of Education, 1954.

ARNOLD, M. R. "An Assault on 'Professionalism.'" *National Observer,* April 13, 1970, p. 10.

AULD, R. B. "The Cooperative Education Movement—Early Years." *Journal of Cooperative Education,* May 1971, pp. 7–9.

BARBEAU, J. E. "The History of the Cooperative Education Movement in American Higher Education." Unpublished doctoral dissertation, Boston University, 1972.

BARBEAU, J. E. "The Spirit of Man: The Educational Philosophy of Dean Schneider." *Journal of Cooperative Education,* May 1971, pp. 1–5.

BARLOW, M. *A Survey of Junior College Work Experience Education Programs.* Los Angeles: Division of Vocational Education, UCLA, 1963.

BARNETT, R., AND STRANDBERG, K. "Student Learning Objectives." Unpublished document from the February 1972 Cooperative Work

Experience Workshop in Anaheim, California, sponsored by the Coast Community College District.

BARON, A. R. *Non-Intellective Variables Related to Successful and Unsuccessful Students in a Junior College.* Washington, D.C.: U.S. Office of Education, 1968.

BENNETT, R., AND REDDING, V. *First Annual Report on Community College Vocational Cooperative Education.* Washington, D.C.: U.S. Office of Education, 1971.

BENNETT, R., AND REDDING, V. *Combined Fifth and Sixth Quarterly Reports on Community College Vocational Cooperative Education.* Washington, D.C.: U.S. Office of Education, 1972.

BENNETT, R. L., AND REDDING, V. *Community College Vocational Cooperative Education, Second Annual Report.* Washington, D.C.: U.S. Office of Education, 1972.

BENNETT, R. L. *Cooperative Education at the College of San Mateo.* Los Angeles: ERIC Clearinghouse for Junior Colleges, 1968.

BENNETT, R. L. *Educational Work Experience in Cooperative Education.* San Mateo, Calif.: Action Link Publishing Company, 1973.

BENNETT, R. L. *Cooperative Education in the San Mateo Junior College District.* Los Angeles: ERIC Clearinghouse for Junior Colleges, 1970.

BENNETT, R. L. "New Opportunities Through Coordinated Instruction Systems." *Junior College Journal.* March 1972, pp. 20–23.

BENNETT, R. L. *Cooperative Distributive Education, An Alternative Semester Program.* Sacramento: Bureau of Cooperative Education, California State Department of Education, 1968.

BIESTER, J. L. "Variations in Off-Campus Programs." *Journal of Cooperative Education,* March 1970, pp. 53–57.

BILLINGS, D. *Cooperative Occupational Education Programs—A Conference Seminar to Extend the Range of Vocational Education Fund Report.* New York: City University of New York, 1970.

BILLINGS, E. R. *Cooperative Education.* Outline of a speech presented to the Sixth Annual Conference of Presidents of the North Carolina Community Junior Colleges, July 1971.

BINZEN, P. H. "LaGuardia Community College, Education in the World of Work." *Change,* February 1973, pp. 35–37.

BLOCKER, C. E., PLUMMER, R. H., AND RICHARDSON, R. G. *The Two-Year College: A Social Synthesis.* Englewood Cliffs, N.J.: Prentice-Hall, Inc., 1965.

BONNELL, A. T. "The Academic Soundness of Cooperative Education." *Journal of Cooperative Education,* November 1964, pp. 19–27.

BOSTWICK, W. D. "Provocative Thoughts about the Coordinator." *Journal of Cooperative Education,* May 1972, pp. 49–51.

BOYER, M. *Cooperative Work-Experience Education Programs in Junior Colleges.* Washington, D.C.: American Association of Junior Colleges, 1970.

BROWN, R. L. *Cooperative Education.* Washington, D.C.: American Association of Junior Colleges, 1972.

BUTLER, R. L., AND YORK, E. G. *What Teacher-Coordinators Should Know About Cooperative Vocational Education.* Columbus, Ohio: ERIC Clearinghouse for Vocational and Technical Education, 1971.

CHAPMAN, E. N. *Work Experience Survival Kit.* Pacific Palisades, Calif.: Goodyear Publishing Company, 1973.

CHASE, J. A. "Research Report: Program Characteristics." *Journal of Cooperative Education,* May 1971, pp. 49–52.

CHASE, J. A. "A Call for Professional Preparation of the College Coordinator." *Journal of Cooperative Education,* November 1968, pp. 8–11.

COHEN, A. M., AND BRAWER, F. B. "The Community College In Search of Identity." *Change,* Winter 1971–1972, pp. 55–59.

COHEN, A. M., AND BRAWER, F. B. "Evaluating Faculty." *Change,* Community College Edition, September 1972, pp. 33a–33d.

COHEN, A. M. *Dateline '79: Heretical Concepts for the Community College.* Beverly Hills: Glencoe Press, 1969.

COHEN, A. M., AND ASSOCIATES. *A Constant Variable.* San Francisco: Jossey-Bass, Inc., 1971.

COHEN, A. M., AND BRAWER, F. B. *Confronting Identity.* Englewood Cliffs, N.J.: Prentice-Hall, Inc., 1972.

COHEN, A. C. *Human Services Institutes, An Alternative for Professional Higher Education.* New York: College for Human Services, 1970.

COHEN, A. C. *The College for Human Services, A New Concept in Professional Higher Education for Low Income Adults.* New York: College for Human Services, 1970.

COLLINS, S. B. "Cooperative Education—Promises and Pitfalls." *Journal of Cooperative Education,* May 1973, pp. 6–9.

COLLINS, S. "Types of Programs." In Asa S. Knowles and Associates, *Handbook of Cooperative Education.* San Francisco: Jossey-Bass, 1971.

CRAWFORD, L. C. *A Competency Pattern Approach to Curriculum Instruction in Distributive Teacher Education.* Blacksburg, Virginia: Virginia Polytechnic Institute, 1969.

CUSHMAN, H. R. *The Concerns and Expectations of Prospective Participants in Directed Work Experience Programs.* Ithaca, New York: State University of New York, 1967.

DAWSON, J. D. *How Cooperative Education can Enhance Special Services Programs for Disadvantaged Students in Colleges and Universities.* Unpublished document, December 1970.

DAWSON, J. D. *Faculty Involvement in Cooperative Education.* Unpublished document, April 1972.

DAWSON, J. D. "College Goals for Cooperative Education." *Journal of Cooperative Education,* May 1973, pp. 1–5.

DAWSON, J. D. *New Directions for Cooperative Education.* New York: National Commission for Cooperative Education, April 1971.

DAWSON, J. D. Unpublished manuscript, "Community and Junior College Cooperative Education Programs." Later modified for a chapter in Asa S. Knowles and Associates, *Handbook of Cooperative Education.* San Francisco: Jossey-Bass, 1971.

DAWSON, J. D. *New Directions for Cooperative Education.* Speech presented to the Insurance Directors Society's annual convention, June 1972.

DAWSON, J. W. *The Masters College Program.* Yellow Springs, Ohio: Union for Experimenting Colleges and Universities, 1971.

Directory of Cooperative Education, 1973. Drexel University, Philadelphia: The Cooperative Education Association, 1973.

DIXON, J. P., AND BUSH, D. "College and the World of Work." *Educational Leadership,* January 1966, pp. 321–329.

DOPP, J., AND NICHOLSON, A. *Guidelines to Cooperative Vocational Education in Community Colleges.* Olympia, Wash.: Washington State Board for Community College Education and Washington State Coordination Council for Occupational Education, n.d.

DUBÉ, P. E. "Cooperative Education in the Social Sciences and Humanities for Colleges Implementing New Programs." *Journal of Cooperative Education,* May 1971, p. 18.

Education Daily, August 4, 1972.

EELLS, W. C. *The Junior College.* Cambridge, Mass.: Riverside Press, 1931.

FAGER, M. K. "Cooperative Education Needs Help in Strengthening

Placement Image." *Journal of Cooperative Education,* November 1969, pp. 35–38.

FARRELL, J. T. "A Job that Buys a Dream." *American Education,* October 1965, pp. 1–4.

FAY, J. *"Coordination"—The Key to Effective Distributive Education Programs.* Speech presented to the American Vocational Association's 61st Annual Convention, December 1967.

FORGEY, G. W. "Work Really Does Pay Off." *Community and Junior College Journal,* February 1973, p. 52.

FREUND, C. J. "The Co-op in the World of Work." *Journal of Cooperative Education,* May 1972, pp. 27–34.

GORE, G. "New Evidence of Co-op System Relevancy." *Journal of Cooperative Education,* May 1972, pp. 7–14.

Grahm Junior College Retail Internship Program. Boston: Grahm Junior College, 1971–1972.

Grahm Junior College Hotel-Motel Internship Program. Boston: Grahm Junior College, 1971–1972.

HALLSTROM, R. "Organizing Cooperative Programs with Industry." In *Selected Papers from Northern Illinois University Community College Conference.* De Kalb, Ill.: Northern Illinois University, 1968.

HARRIS, N. *Technical Education in the Junior College: New Programs for New Jobs,* Washington, D.C.: American Association of Junior Colleges, 1964.

HATCHER, H. "Comments on College Cooperative Education." *Journal of Cooperative Education,* April 1967, pp. 1–7.

HAYES, G. *Junior College Work Experience Education.* Los Angeles: ERIC Clearinghouse for Junior Colleges, 1969.

HAYES, G. E. *"Work Experience Education Programs—Innovation in the Junior College Curricula."* Los Angeles: ERIC Junior College Clearinghouse, 1969.

HEERMANN, B., AND PUTHOFF, J. *Contact Grade Report for Occupational Education Students.* Based on a similar report requirement used by the Ohio State University Distributive Education Department, Neal Vivian. Sinclair Community College, Dayton, Ohio.

HORN, H. H. "Cooperative Education—Key to Transition to Industry." *Engineering Education,* April 1971, pp. 795–797.

HUBER, P. M. "A Summary of the Critical Requirements for the Coordinator in College Cooperative Education Programs." *Journal of Cooperative Education,* November 1971, pp. 20–30.

HUFFMAN, H., editor. *Guidelines in Cooperative Education*. Columbus, Ohio: Center for Vocational and Technical Education, 1967.

HUNT, D. "And It Happened This Way." *Journal of Cooperative Education*, November 1964, pp. 3–4.

HUNT, D. C. "Relations with Private Employers." In Asa S. Knowles and Associates, *Handbook of Cooperative Education*. San Francisco: Jossey-Bass, 1971.

INGRAM, J. F. "What Makes Education Vocational?" *American School Board Journal*, November 1956, pp. 1–5, reprint.

JOHNSON, B. L. *Islands of Innovation Expanding: Changes in the Community College*. Beverly Hills: Glencoe Press, 1969.

KELLY, W., AND WILBUR, L. *Teaching in the Community Junior College*. New York: Appleton-Century-Crofts, 1970.

KLEIN, W., DENHAM, W., AND FISHMAN, J. *New Careers: A Manual of Organization and Development*. Washington, D.C.: New Careers Institute, University Research Corporation, 1968.

KNOWLES, A. K. "Is Cooperative Education the Answer?" *The Conference Board Record*, January 1971.

KNOWLES, A. S. "General Administration." In Asa S. Knowles and Associates, *Handbook for Cooperative Education*. San Francisco: Jossey-Bass, Inc., 1971.

KNOWLES, A., AND WOOLDRIDGE, R. "The Adoption of Cooperative Education." In Asa S. Knowles and Associates, *Handbook of Cooperative Education*. San Francisco: Jossey-Bass, 1971.

KNOWLES, A. "Future of Cooperative Education." In Asa S. Knowles and Associates, *Handbook of Cooperative Education*. San Francisco: Jossey-Bass, 1971.

KNOWLES, A. "Academic Administration." In Asa S. Knowles and Associates, *Handbook of Cooperative Education*. San Francisco: Jossey-Bass, 1971.

KOOS, L. *The Community College Student*. Gainesville, Fla.: University of Florida, 1970.

KUHN, L. F. "Four Facets of Co-op Program Operation." *Journal of Cooperative Education*, November 1968, pp. 42–45.

Lees Junior College Bulletin, 1971–1972. Jackson, Ky.: Lees Junior College, 1971.

LENTZ, G. F., AND SELIGSOHN, H. C. "Co-op Versus Regular Student Attitudes." *Journal of Cooperative Education*, November 1968, pp. 27–32.

LEUBA, C. *Effective Learning and Cooperative Education*. New York: National Commission for Cooperative Education, 1964.

LINDENMEYER, R. S. "A Comparison Study of the Academic Progress of the Cooperative and the Four-Year Student." *Journal of Cooperative Education,* April 1967, pp. 8–17.

LUPTON, D. K. "The Coop Mandate for College Work-Study Programs." *Journal of Cooperative Education,* May 1970, pp. 39–43.

LUPTON, D. K., AND WADSWORTH, R. B. "Junior College Co-op: Partnership and Practice." *Journal of Cooperative Education,* May 1969, pp. 50–57.

LUPTON, D. K. "Communications in Co-op Field Supervision." *Journal of Cooperative Education,* May 1972, p. 40.

LUPTON, D. K. "The Employer's Role in Cooperative Education." *Journal of Cooperative Education,* November 1969, pp. 51–56.

LUPTON, D. K. "Campus-Stretching Through Cooperative Education." *Junior College Journal,* February 1970, pp. 37–39.

LUPTON, D. K. *The Student in Society.* Totawa, N.J.: Littlefield, Adams and Company, 1969.

LUPTON, D. K., AND MC NUTT, D. E. "Academic Credit for Cooperative Education." *Journal of Cooperative Education,* November 1972, pp. 60–65.

MAGER, R. F. *Preparing Instructional Objectives.* Palo Alto, California: Fearon Publishers, 1962.

MAGER, R. F., AND BEACH, K. M., JR. *Developing Vocational Instruction.* Palo Alto, California: Fearon Publishers, 1967.

MARKS, E., AND WOHLFORD, J. "The Co-op Experience and Its Effect on Undergraduates." *Engineering Education,* April 1971, pp. 822–824.

MARKS, M. V. "Improving Occupational Experiences Through Coordinated Classroom Experiences." *Business Education Forum,* April 1963, pp. 5–7.

MARTIN, A. " 'Radical' College Aiding City Slums." *New York Times,* November 29, 1970.

MASON, R. E., AND HAINES, P. G. *Cooperative Occupational Education.* Danville, Ill.: Interstate Printers and Publishers, 1972. Second edition

MC KINNEY, L. M. "Minority Students." In Asa S. Knowles and Associates, *Handbook of Cooperative Education.* San Francisco: Jossey-Bass, 1971.

MEDSKER, L. F. *The Junior College: Progress and Prospect.* New York: McGraw-Hill, 1960.

MEYER, W., KLAURENS, M., AND ASHMAN, R. *A Guide for Cooperative*

Vocational Education. Minneapolis: University of Minnesota, Division of Vocational and Technical Education, May 1969.

Miami-Dade Junior College, South Campus. Description of "Career Orientation Workshop," 1971.

MICHELSON, G. G. "New Dimensions for Co-ops in Non-Engineering Areas." *Journal of Cooperative Education,* May 1970, pp. 16–21.

MILLER, G. H. "Relations with Students." In Asa S. Knowles and Associates, *Handbook of Cooperative Education.* San Francisco: Jossey-Bass, 1971.

MOSBACKER, W. B. "The Role of the Coordinator." *Journal of Cooperative Education,* May 1969, pp. 29–37.

OPPERMAN, D. R. "The Case for Academic Credit in Cooperative Education," *Engineering Education,* April 1971, pp. 800–802.

PEARL, A., AND RIESSMAN, F. *New Careers for the Poor: The Non-professionals in Human Service.* New York: The Free Press, 1965.

PETTEBONE, E. R. "Co-op as a Basis for Credit." *Journal of Cooperative Education,* November 1971, pp. 8–10.

PLACHTA, L. "The Role of the Teacher in Cooperative Education." *Journal of Cooperative Education,* May 1969, pp. 18–20.

PORTMAN, D. N. *The Work Study Program in Higher Education.* Syracuse, N.Y.: Syracuse University, 1970.

PRATT, C. G. L. "Personal Counseling—Within the Realm of the Coordinator?" *Journal of Cooperative Education,* May 1972, pp. 46–52.

PRICE, R. M. "Today's Story of Cooperative Education Practices and Previews." *Journal of Cooperative Education,* November 1968, pp. 33–35.

PROBST, G. E. "Promotion and Exchange of Information." In Asa S. Knowles and Associates, *Handbook of Cooperative Education.* San Francisco: Jossey-Bass, 1971.

RAUH, M. A. *The Advantages of Work-Study Plans.* New York: The Academy for Educational Development, 1971.

REDDING, V. N., GARMAN, J. E., AND STRANDBERG, K. S. *A Manual for Students in Cooperative Education.* Costa Mesa, California: Orange Coast College, 1971.

Resource Manual 71 for the Development of Cooperative Vocational Education Programs. Washington, D.C.: Division of Vocational and Technical Education, U.S. Office of Education, 1971.

ROBERTS, R. W. *Vocational and Practical Arts Education: History,*

Development, and Principles. New York: Harper and Row, 1965.

Rock Valley College Career Advancement Program. Rockford, Illinois: Rock Valley College, 1968.

ROWE, P. M., AND LUMLEY, C. "Changes In Job Satisfaction for Successive Work Terms." *Journal of Cooperative Education,* November 1971, pp. 10–15.

ROWE, P. M. "Motivation and Job Satisfaction on the Work Term of Cooperative Students." *Journal of Cooperative Education,* November 1970, pp. 13–23.

SAMSON, H. E. *The Nature and Characteristics of Middle Management in Retail Department Stores.* Madison, Wis.: University of Wisconsin Distributive Education Resource Center, 1969.

SCHUETZ, C. Merritt College Cooperative Education Meeting, April 28, 1972. Mimeographed report of meeting.

"Self-Made College." *Time,* July 6, 1970.

SEAVERNS, C. F., JR. *A Manual for Coordinators of Cooperative Education.* Boston: Center for Cooperative Education, Northeastern University, 1970.

SMITH, H. S. "The Influence of Participation in the Cooperative Program on Academic Performance." *Journal of Cooperative Education,* November 1965, pp. 7–17.

SMITH, M. D. "Co-op Education." *Open Door,* Summer 1970, pp. 11–13.

THORNTON, J. W., JR. *The Community Junior College.* New York: Wiley, 1966.

TYLER, R. W. "Values and Objectives." In Asa S. Knowles and Associates, *Handbook of Cooperative Education.* San Francisco: Jossey-Bass, 1971.

VAN SICKLE, H. "Professional Development of Women." In Asa S. Knowles and Associates, *Handbook of Cooperative Education.* San Francisco: Jossey-Bass, 1971.

VENN, G. *Selected Papers.* Washington, D.C.: American Association of Junior Colleges, 1967.

VENN, G. *Man, Education, and Work.* Washington: American Council on Education, 1964.

VENN, G. *Programs in Two-Year Colleges to Up-Grade Employees of Business and Industry.* Washington, D.C.: American Association of Junior Colleges. 1969.

VICKREY, J. F., JR., AND MILLER, G. H. "Co-op Education and University Relations—Cooperative in Education." *Journal of Cooperative Education,* May 1973, pp. 9–18.

WALLACE, H. R. *Review and Synthesis of Research on Cooperative Vocational Education.* Columbus, Ohio: ERIC Clearinghouse on Vocational and Technical Education, 1970.

WATSON, N. E. "Corporations and Community Colleges: A Growing Liaison?" *Technical Education News,* April-May 1970, pp. 3–6.

"Where All Education is Cooperative." *College Management,* May 1972, pp. 17–18.

WILSON, J. W., AND LYONS, E. H. *Work-Study College Programs.* New York: Harper, 1961.

WILSON, J. W. "On the Nature of Cooperative Education." *Journal of Cooperative Education,* May 1970, pp. 1–10.

WILSON, J. W. "Cooperative Education and Degree Credit." *Journal of Cooperative Education,* May 1973, pp. 28–38.

WILSON, J. W. "Federal Funding for Cooperative Education, Report and Suggestions." *Journal of Cooperative Education,* May 1971, pp. 43–49.

WILSON, J. W. "Survey of Cooperative Education, 1970." *Journal of Cooperative Education,* November 1970, pp. 31–44.

WILSON, J. W. "Survey of Cooperative Education, 1971." *Journal of Cooperative Education,* November 1971, pp. 39–51.

WILSON, J. W. "Survey of Cooperative Education, 1972." *Journal of Cooperative Education,* November 1972, pp. 9–15.

WILSON, J. "Historical Development." In Asa S. Knowles and Associates, *Handbook of Cooperative Education.* San Francisco: Jossey-Bass, 1971.

WILSON, J. W. "Growth and Current Status of Cooperative Engineering Education." *Engineering Education,* April 1971, pp. 790–794.

WILSON, J. W. "Reflections on What a Coordinator Is." *Journal of Cooperative Education,* May 1972, pp. 59–60.

WILSON, J. W. "A Study of Coordinator Beliefs About the Student-Coordinator Relationship." *Journal of Cooperative Education,* November 1969, pp. 43–50.

WOOLDRIDGE, R. L. *Cooperative Education and the Community College in New Jersey.* New York: The National Commission for Cooperative Education, 1966.

WOOLDRIDGE, R. L. "The Development of Cooperative Education in the United States." *Journal of Cooperative Education,* November 1964, pp. 10–17.

Index

A

Administration: centralized, 67-72, 74-78; of cooperative education programs, 51-65; decentralized, 67-68, 72-74, 77-79; organization of, 66-84; as problem, 47-49; role of, 32-33, 162-163

ALCOR, 159

Alice Lloyd College, 158

ALLEN, J. E., JR., 154-155

Alternating block plan: advantages of, 108; financial aspects of, 56-57; in operation of cooperative education, 31-32; schedules for, 112; training plan in, 106; and trimester, 111

American Vocational Association: membership in, 5; and vocational education values, 13

Antioch College, 4, 9, 11

Associations of cooperative educators, 5-7

Attrition, 37, 39

AULD, R. B., 4, 205

B

BARBEAU, J. E., 4, 5, 205

BARLOW, M., 45, 46, 48, 49, 81, 87, 205

BARNETT, R., 130-131, 205, 206

BARON, A. R., 37, 206

BEACH, K. M., JR., 135, 211

BENNETT, R., 8, 40, 58, 110, 131, 133, 139, 156, 157, 159, 203, 206

BIESTER, J. L., 12, 206

BILLINGS, D., 45, 47, 48, 49, 58, 59-60, 82-83, 206

BILLINGS, E. R., 45, 153, 206

BLOCKER, C. E., 2, 206

BONNELL, A. T., 45, 46, 47, 207

BOSTWICK, W. D., 74, 89, 207

BRAWER, F. B., 2, 58, 207

Broward Community College: career orientation class at, 140; student handbook at, 153

213